Daryl Balia is a native South Afri
theology and public administrati
minister, was an associate professoi
and was Chief Director of Ethics
He is now the International Direc... .. .. a research
project in missiology, which is based at New College, University of
Edinburgh.

MAKE CORRUPTION HISTORY

DARYL BALIA

First published in Great Britain in 2009

Society for Promoting Christian Knowledge
36 Causton Street
London SW1P 4ST

The author and publisher have made every effort to ensure that the external
website and email addresses included in this book are correct and up to date at
the time of going to press. The author and publisher are not responsible for the
content, quality or continuing accessibility of the sites.

Scripture quotations are translated by the author.

British Library Cataloguing-in-Publication Data
A catalogue record for this book is available from the British Library

ISBN 978–0–281–06030–6

1 3 5 7 9 10 8 6 4 2

Typeset by Graphicraft Ltd, Hong Kong
Printed in Great Britain by Ashford Colour Press

Produced on paper from sustainable forests

Contents

Acknowledgements

My family deserve to be acknowledged first for having given me their permission, often grudgingly, to ignore them at critical times and focus instead on writing this book. Little Tarah was born just when I had completed my doctoral thesis in public management, from which this study draws heavily. Both she and, to a lesser extent, Javahl and Rosita as well, have suffered, I suppose, from my time away from them. My colleagues at the University of South Africa, Koos Pauw and Kobus Wessels, were very supportive when I began research work on corruption under their direction in 2002. The Office of the Public Service Commission in Pretoria provided me, as an employee there from 1998 to 2004, with an almost perfect environment within which to gain significant insights into the operations of all tiers of government, especially those engaged in work against corruption. Similarly, as chairperson of the board for Transparency International South Africa, I was able to place myself strategically at critical events and among key people, locally and abroad, who knew more than I did about how best to tackle corruption. I learned much from them, inasmuch as my work in good governance was inspired by the fellowship I was privileged to enjoy with colleagues, among them Jeremy Pope, Stuart Gilman, Hennie van Vuuren and Howard Whitton. Leslie Griffiths continues to be an inspiration to Christians everywhere in giving his prophetic ministry such a public face and I am honoured that he has agreed to introduce the subject at hand to readers. Rebecca Mulhearn from SPCK deserves special mention for her patience with me in not meeting her deadlines, among my other sins of omission. In the midst of finishing some of the drafts for the publisher my mother passed away and so I dedicate this book to her memory, appropriately enough as I cannot recall her ever having told a lie!

Foreword

'Make corruption history' – a brilliant title for a subject that should command our attention. Even though, as Daryl Balia shows us, this is a subject that's been formally before us for a relatively short time, it's been prowling around (like the Devil himself!) for a long time seeking whom it may devour. So I'm delighted to introduce this important study to what I hope will be a wide readership.

I lived in Haiti throughout the 1970s and was about to begin to address the question of corruption out of my experiences there. Haiti ranks 177th out of 180 in the Transparency International league table, with only Iraq, Myanmar and Somalia beneath it! So it's obviously a reasonable place to start.

But then I checked myself. As it happens, I'm writing this at a time of great economic uncertainty. The international financial system has been in trouble for months now and we'll not really know either the full extent or the true causes of it until historians begin the task of gathering information at some future date. But we can already detect a number of factors. The drive for quick profits led many banks and other similar institutions to offer credit on terms that were ridiculously easy. They then proceeded to share the risks of these ventures on a global scale. So something that began in the United States of America, the sub-prime mortgage market, was soon to have worldwide ramifications.

Meanwhile, very clever people in the financial sector were devising intricate products that were far too sophisticated for their own top management to understand. Pure, unadulterated greed drove those running our financial institutions to drive up profits in order to create huge bonuses that had little or nothing to do with the real effort involved. Hedge funds were selling short in order to make big gains. We were told, *ad nauseam*, that this was a very legitimate way of giving themselves space to make a deal. To ordinary people, however, it all felt like betting on failure.

When Nick Leeson fooled everybody in 1995 with a resultant loss to his bank of £827 million, we thought our financiers would take fright. When, later, Northern Rock was proved to have been too adventurous by far in its lending policies, we assumed it was an exception to the rule. But Jérôme Kerviel at the Banque de Paris made losses of €4.9 billion before anyone discovered what he was up to. And Bernie Madoff managed to cook his books to the extent of $50 billion before he meekly owned up.

With all this in mind, how could I possibly start to examine corruption in poor old Haiti, which has little or nothing in the way of assets to work with, while remaining silent about the things I see all around me every single day? It would have been tantamount to seeing the speck in the eye of a failed state while ignoring the two short planks sticking out of the eyes of the 'developed world'.

Insider dealing, asset stripping, short-termism – these have been hanging in the air we breathe for a very long time. If we take Daryl Balia's definition of corruption ('the misuse of public office for private gain') as our starting point, it's not difficult to pin all kinds of accusations upon some of the most powerful people in the world. And their behaviour, far from merely dragging an undeveloped country down the drain, is risking the collapse of the world financial order as we know it.

Another thing that's happening as I compose this introduction is the scandal in the House of Lords surrounding the sale of 'influence'. That is, people with titles have been accused by a newspaper of attempting to shape and direct public policy by taking cash for laying down amendments to pieces of legislation currently being debated. This led to the almost unprecedented suspension of two members of the House. And this is only the latest of a number of dubious practices in both the British Houses of Parliament. The public outrage at the revelations surrounding MPs' expenses has led to insistent calls for a root and branch reform of our whole parliamentary system. These events would certainly qualify for consideration under the definition of corruption offered in this book.

Having got that off my chest, I can now feel more comfortable looking at Haiti. Even so, I don't want to dwell on what is only too obvious. The Haitian government of Jean-Claude Duvalier entertained the idea of undertaking massive development projects (funded by various agencies of the United Nations) on the strict condition that every single foreign technocrat employed by such projects had to be matched by a 'homologue' of Haitian nationality. Since these experts were highly paid and the Haitian counterpart was to receive exactly the same as the foreigner, this doubled the top management costs of every single project at a stroke. It allowed the government to enjoy patronage and it meant, almost inevitably, the failure of every single project. It was no wonder to me that, one bright day in London, a top official from Washington contacted me to tell me about a 'cry session' he'd just come from in the United States. All those who had in any way been involved in running projects in Haiti over the previous ten years came together for 36 hours. They gave each other permission to tell their stories of failure. It was recognized that the untold millions of dollars that had been pumped into aid and development projects in Haiti had come to nothing. Absolutely nothing. It had been a moment of sheer devastation to the officials gathered in Washington DC.

Throughout the 1970s, I became accustomed to seeing Haitians queue to sell blood to American teaching hospitals (this was before the HIV/AIDS crisis broke on us all). And I was only too familiar with the plight of young boys and girls selling their little bodies to rich tourists. I was aware from my own work of the prevalence of preventable disease – gangrene, secondary syphilis, tuberculosis and malaria. It wouldn't have needed much organization or capital investment to address those needs. But none was forthcoming. Yet government officials and placemen were becoming fabulously rich before our wondering eyes.

In the agricultural sector, meanwhile, things were going from bad to worse. Droughts and floods and hurricanes and earthquakes seemed to follow each other in rapid succession. When US wheat began to be dumped on the Haitian market, it meant the end of the Haitian rice production programme. In a decade, Haiti went from being able to feed itself to being totally dependent on external sources for basic food stuffs.

I mention all this because any understanding of corruption in Haiti has to be predicated upon an understanding of how deep is the poverty of its people. Seven million inhabitants live in a country the size of Wales (which itself has a mere two million). The land is rough and inhospitable. Because of centuries of deforestation, with trees felled for building and fuel, there has been too an impoverishment of the soil and denudation of the terrain. Is it any wonder, therefore, that people scramble around for whatever advantage they can find? Can we label the survival skills of people who face ruin and starvation on a daily basis with the word 'corruption'? Or should we admire them for their ingenuity and persistence? The question deserves discussion.

Daryl Balia offers an exhaustive study of his native South Africa and I have found this most instructive. Its insights should challenge the thinking of everyone who reads these pages. But I feel bound to say that beyond countries like South Africa lie the basket cases of countries like Haiti. And in such countries a new raft of criteria must enter into play. For many years now I have felt that the United Nations Trusteeship Council, a body which thought it had finished its work, needs to be revived. There are nations which need to be taken in hand, given the space to develop leadership and to create civil society, as a necessary precondition to shaping governments that can in any known way be held to be transparent and accountable. That too, it seems to me, is a debate worth having.

Let me end on an entirely different note. During the decade I lived in Haiti, I found myself involved in a whole range of responses to people's needs. There were schools and literacy programmes, we sank wells and built roads, we formed co-operatives, desalinated seawater, established irrigation systems on otherwise barren land. We planted trees. We ran a mobile clinic and offered primary healthcare to scattered rural communities. We put feeding programmes together. We gave people opportunity both for creative activity and for recreation and distraction. All of this was done on a shoestring. And in its totality, it made a serious response to the proven needs of the Haitian people.

I was in Haiti as a Christian missionary. Only when I could speak both of Haiti's languages fluently and had endured some of the hardships known to its inhabitants, did I feel 'qualified' to offer leadership. I looked askance at foreigners who came and, on the basis of five minutes' knowledge, offered their 'expert' advice. Among the very first things I sought to do was to build a leadership team – a group of Haitian people who met regularly to plan and develop the work we were doing. It was also important for me to know that, at my departure, the work we were doing had a chance of continuing on its way. Sustainability was written in to our efforts.

We resisted the blandishments and the financial offers made to us by many organizations. They saw the way we were doing our work and wanted to muscle in on it. I refused to entertain the idea of 'sponsoring' individual children. I shunned offers of help that came with 'strings' attached. We avoided undue sophistication. Our work was simplicity itself. Everybody was treated with dignity and as proper human beings.

How could a Christian work in any other way? If God had taken humanity seriously enough to identify with it in the most costly way imaginable, then surely human beings purporting to act in his name must themselves be ready to identify themselves in total integrity with the people among whom they work. There's no room for paternalism or exploitation, no excuse for ripping people off or humiliating them. Their plight is already serious enough without such barbarous ways of behaving.

Without continuing this description any further, I am glad to offer it as an antidote to corruption. When people are treated with dignity, when they can hold on to hope, when they see their crops grow and know that they stand a chance of remaining healthy, when their children are educated and they have time to laugh and have fun together, then the law of the jungle stands a chance of being replaced by the law of decent humanity.

This is being written at the time when we are celebrating the 200th anniversary of the birth of Charles Darwin. In the economic order as well as within the worlds of biology and nature, the struggle for survival is only too evident. Only the fittest will make it. Where poverty and inequality and injustice reign, it's no wonder to me that corruption flourishes. The real challenge to us all is to end poverty. That will always have to be a number one priority. But we are where we are. Corruption and graft abound. They short-cut the process of building a fair and decent world. They enter the cultural bloodstream and carry infection to the furthest extremes of the body politic. So we have to find a way to mount a twin-track policy of attrition, to fight a war on two fronts. Daryl Balia has done us all a great service in laying bare the inner workings of corruption. What follows should be essential reading for anyone seeking to do what the Lord requires of us – to act justly, to love mercy, and to walk humbly with God.

Lord Griffiths of Burry Port

Introduction

Over the past two decades, corruption has increasingly become a matter of global concern and a subject for serious study. The advent of the internet and other new technologies, unprecedented economic activity around the world, the opening up of borders and the removal of barriers to facilitate trade, increased capital flows, and the almost toxic spread of consumer culture have all led to more opportunities to engage in corrupt practices. Organized criminal networks have also as a result become active, at times operating in cahoots with elected leaders. The richer nations of the world, while reputedly less corrupt, have greatly contributed to the malaise by failing to deal harshly with the guilty. In some cases, corporations have been given tax deductions for bribes paid abroad, while corrupt governments have been given loans. Funds looted from state coffers are allowed to sit in secret bank accounts while the poor are the ones who suffer the most. Given the impact of corruption in Africa, many of its people have suffered inexorably at the hands of its leaders, but also through bribery practices involving multinational companies.

We should note at the outset that the debate about corruption is mostly fuelled from the demand side, that is, government corruption at the country level with its negative economic impact on poverty and development. The supply side, where employees of large corporations pay bribes usually to win government contracts, is given secondary interest. Most of the proceeds from corrupt activities originate from a diversion of resources meant to serve the people's needs, thus undermining the struggle against poverty. Such corruption thrives in places where little respect is given to human rights and the values of transparency and accountability are frowned upon. Democratic culture is put at great risk when corruption becomes so endemic that a government's ability to govern is compromised. Though the phenomenon has been with us from time immemorial, it is only since the 1990s that the world has awakened to a new awareness of the corrosive impact of corruption on human behaviour.

The impact of corruption on good governance, its extent and the potential of various measures to reduce it are usually given wide

xiii

coverage. Very little has been written about it from a Christian point of view, nor has the role, relevance and priority of funding the effort of fighting corruption been given much attention.[1] The countries of the world most prone to endemic corruption are usually the ones most in need of assistance. Without such help, and a calculation of the costs of combating corruption and the benefits this should eventually bring to society, our best efforts to make a positive impact will be thwarted. Most governments remain committed to reducing corruption in all sectors of public life, yet such commitment is often voiced merely for public consumption and is not translated into providing the necessary funding to do so. Political leaders are noted for their pious prattling against corruption, but are reluctant to commit substantial resources towards its control. This might be due to a faulty analysis of the problem of corruption and its corrosive impact on society generally. It is a misconception to assume that we can afford to 'fight' corruption 'at all costs', or, for that matter, adopt a policy of 'zero tolerance' towards it. Our attempt will therefore be to show that a developing country cannot actually afford to budget for a zero tolerance approach, and that the costs of fighting corruption must be balanced against the benefits that this is likely to bring society. The struggle against corruption should consequently not be directed towards its total elimination, as this of itself is not possible. The aim should be to ensure that a carefully formulated strategic approach is adopted which must be based on the ability of a country to harness available resources, human capacity and political will. As corruption is as much a question of reality as it is of perception, evaluating the impact of efforts to fight corruption requires that tangible benefits accrue to the citizenry such that public confidence in a government's ability to govern is bolstered.

Sometimes we observe how additional resources to combat corruption are inappropriately committed, resulting in a lack of coherent implementation and little impact. Political immaturity and lack of foresight can also cause key decisions to be rashly taken, severely tarnishing a country's record of fighting corruption. One country in particular is chosen to illustrate the complexity surrounding the problem of corruption: South Africa. South Africa's programmatic attempts since 1997 to confront corruption compare favourably with those of other African countries like Botswana and might offer a best-practice model for some developing countries. Still, the absence of management controls, adequate information, overall policy, monitoring mechanisms and effective co-ordination continue to be critical retarding factors, especially on the part of government. All of this diminishes the likelihood of reducing corruption in South Africa. It is in any case imperative that a country's national strategy to fight corruption is fully supported from the top echelons of political authority downwards, so as to instil confidence among all citizens that government is united in its concern to address the problem. Under the moral leadership provided by President Nelson Mandela, South Africa was to make significant advances in recognizing the urgent need to tackle corruption in the midst of other political challenges.

South Africa is a useful case study that can illuminate the relevant issues and problems and provide insight into phenomena that cannot be observed directly. We can also test some of our propositions against what has happened in South Africa and can estimate the consequences (or the costs and benefits) of various alternative courses of action. Real life cases are a more reliable basis for policy choices than subjective judgments provided, of course, that they can be tested.[2] In this book it may prove useful to examine briefly the models of fighting corruption that have been advanced in the relevant literature and compare them with the approach often adopted whereby the public policymaking process produces the ideal policy for a target group (those impacted the most by the policy) and it is implemented by a responsible agency (usually of government). Usually, various 'environmental factors' (such as the scope and limits of transparency, accountability, efficacy, etc., being made inherent in a policy framework) affect the policymaking process, causing tensions and conflicts which in turn give rise to varying responses by institutions and other role-players, thus influencing future policymaking.[3]

While the costs of corruption itself, its effects on poverty reduction or human rights violations, for example, are extensively mentioned and studied, usually for measurement's sake, little attention has been given to calculating the costs of fighting corruption. This might seem odd to the casual observer, but not if one considers the political import that public officials attach to their rhetoric against corruption. The attention increasingly being given to the problem of corruption in the developing world by economists has not helped, as their attempts continue to focus on establishing the extent of its negative impact on a country's economy. One is also treated to a plethora of solutions, often informed by public sector experts, but which mostly fail to address the dearth of leadership and lack of resources that hamper the implementation of most anti-corruption plans. Such plans often fail because of political interference, lack of independence, inadequate skills, and poor co-ordination with other state agencies. Here, we seek to highlight the lack of attention given to the issue of providing 'adequate' financial resources, without which it will not be possible to fight corruption effectively. 'Adequate' is of course a relative term contingent upon the availability of resources and the priority given to fighting corruption within a country's budgetary framework. Condemning public sector corruption might be a fashionable preoccupation for many in all spheres of government, but if such rhetoric is not accompanied by a commitment of resources, the fight against corruption will be rendered ineffective.

Many a civil servant will have a tale to tell about the sense of frustration and dissatisfaction experienced when trying to be faithful to the government of the day. On the basis of thorough study and scientific investigation, a civil servant can make recommendations meant to ameliorate a certain problem afflicting society, only to be pushed aside by political actors who share 'broader' concerns related to party loyalty and the need to placate their constituencies. Discussion of competing options to fight corruption can be limited within the governmental environment to the formal programme already in place, with little room and time to explore radical alternatives. The results of a scientific study of corruption can in any case be quite discomforting to those entrenched in positions of power and threatening to those with insecure jobs. However, the task of finding out the best ways to reduce corruption is made more difficult as there is a paucity of studies evaluating the prevalence and practice of corruption from a theological perspective, let alone the measures taken to combat its spread. Christians will ordinarily share a sense of moral outrage towards corrupt behaviour that has had an enormous negative impact on the poor. We read or hear numerous stories of petty corruption involving public officials who never seem to get caught. If and when such officials are eventually disciplined, they seem as a rule to escape criminal prosecution. Such a scenario prevails despite repeated pledges by those in authority to 'come down hard' on those guilty of corruption. Sometimes those showing most public intent to fight corruption turn out to be those implicated in questionable practices. It is difficult, however, to provide adequate solutions to an age-old problem afflicting humankind if one does not fully comprehend the problem itself. All Christians, especially those in government, are ostensibly fervent supporters of action being taken against corruption, except perhaps in certain selected cases when higher interests prevail.

Practical studies on fighting corruption[4] generally put much emphasis on the role of important institutions that, for the purposes of this study, cannot be discussed in any great detail. The independence of parliament and the judiciary are paramount to ensuring transparency and accountability in any society that seeks a reduction in corruption. We must assume that such institutions exist, are quite independent, and contribute in their unique ways to limit the spread of corruption. It is possible to argue that public sector reforms, specifically measures to improve salaries and employment conditions, can contribute towards reduced opportunities for corruption, or that the tax reforms of a country can have the same effect. Some significant studies have appeared which offer new variables to the debate about corruption. One such study robustly claims that it is lower in richer countries, 'where democratic institutions have been preserved for a long continuous period, and the population is mainly Protestant'.[5] Another sees puritanical movements of a fundamentalist hue as offering hope 'in the absence of an improbable self-reformation of the political elites, to attempt to change the present course of affairs'.[6] It should be noted that the focus of this book is not to devise a formula or method to assist any church, aid agency or government to calculate the cost involved in reducing corruption. It is in any case a task of immense difficulty, if it is at all possible, to measure the total costs of fighting corruption when the extent of corruption itself defies measurement. It is possible, however, to use the economic choice model of cost-benefit analysis in the public sector to provide better solutions to the problems of resource allocation and offer methodologies to measure particular categories of costs and benefits (see Chapter 4).[7] In this book we try to draw attention to the priority of moral leadership and costs involved in fighting corruption without going into any detail about its measurement, as this is a complex matter probably requiring a separate study. Our focus will therefore serve to alert churches, aid agencies and mission organizations about the need to join the fight against corruption with a concomitant task of understanding that such an effort must be adequately funded within strategic frameworks for action.

Part 1

UNDERSTANDING CORRUPTION

1

The problem with corruption

Defining 'corruption'

It is desirable at the outset to offer a clear and unambiguous definition of the word 'corruption' in view of its variety of usages and meanings across the world. However, it is not always possible to define exactly what counts as corrupt and what doesn't, and furthermore, it sometimes suits politicians for the boundaries to be blurred.[1] Since elaborate essays have already been written on the question of defining corruption, and as we have no interest in making a case for a new definition, it will suffice to mention the most common understandings of corruption and other related patterns of behaviour.[2] We should note that there has never been anything like overall agreement on the definition of the term since no two writers use the same criteria to arrive at their understanding.[3] When corruption is viewed as a violation of a norm or standard, the question that inevitably arises is whose standard of behaviour is being upheld as the morally correct one. Especially within the cultural milieu, what one person may consider corrupt may be seen by another as perfectly acceptable behaviour. Yet this should not prevent us from using a working definition that, though not valid for all conceivable situations, will be of help in understanding more clearly when, where, why and how corruption takes place and what can possibly be done to contain its spread.

Arnold Heidenheimer, who spent his academic life in the United States, has provided a detailed discussion of the *Oxford English Dictionary*'s list of nine possible meanings of corruption, although interestingly, most do not apply to the political context where the practice of corruption is most often rife. These meanings are categorized into physical, moral and perverting usages. Corruption is therefore the physical 'destruction or spoiling of anything, especially by disintegration or by decomposition with its attendant unwholesomeness and loathsomeness'. But it is also 'a making or becoming morally corrupt, a fact or condition of being corrupt; moral deterioration or decay; depravity', and 'the perversion of an institution, custom, and so forth from its primitive purity'.[4] A strictly legal definition would restrict one to studying only those cases of corruption that can be tried in a court of law and 'it would negate the possibility of investigating a change in the nature of corruption'.[5] Formal norms of conduct in office differ and 'an identical action in two nations will be labelled differently because of differences in laws'.[6] Everything legal is not necessarily ethical. Actions or inactions, which may yet need to be included in one's definition of corruption, will have to be excluded if one follows the legal route. It is also possible for some actions, like nepotism, to be considered corrupt but not usually to be deemed illegal in modern democracies. The employment of family members by politicians, sometimes to work in their own offices, might be a case in point.

In this book we shall use a definition that is quite common among economists, civil society activists and social scientists, namely that corruption is the 'misuse of public office for private gain'. This definition owes its origins to the *Encyclopaedia of the Social Sciences*, where it is observed by Joseph Senturia as 'the misuse of public power for private profit'.[7] Yet, even as Senturia recognized, such a definition is not without its limitations. 'Patriotic corruption', such as taxation by a dictator to bring benefits to himself, for example, or benefits to the public that he may procure through personal vices, is not included in the preferred definition. This usually involves the *use* of public office for private gain in situations of personal rule, kleptocracy (a government characterized by the practice of transferring money and power to the ruling elite at the expense of the citizenry) and prebendalism (where portions of revenue due to the state are held in reserve for payment to selected officials). In these situations the distinction between public and private is weak, and personal relationships are as a norm the basis of the political system. Countries like Haiti and Indonesia have had a history of such types of patriotic corruption. Most instances of corruption, however, as defined by the United Nations Convention Against Corruption (2003) can be subsumed under the operational definition of corruption as the misuse of public office (public power, public interest, public authority) for private gain (private benefit, private profit, personal gain, family or group benefit). If and when the term 'graft' (illicit gain

4

in politics or business) is used, it should also be understood in terms of the above definition of corruption.

Types of corruption

Some related forms of behaviour are also frequently mentioned as acts of corruption and these are worth noting:

- *Bribery* is one very common example, where a public official (often a male) is 'induced' improperly (usually through kickback, speed money, sweeteners) to perform a certain function by a citizen who wants to gain some kind of advantage.
- *Gift giving* is potentially the most common form of corruption. The classic question of course is, when is a gift not a gift? That is, when is a gift given without interest or in a way that does not enhance solidarity? The exercise of public office is meant to be gratuitously performed, but as in most cases of corruption, it is improperly induced by the offer of gifts. 'Gifts' can vary from a simple lunch to an elaborate payment, from a concert invitation to an offer of employment, from a pen to a yacht. Yet as the giving and receiving of gifts is common practice among most cultures, those serving in public office are not exempt. Suspicion will obviously arise if a gift is accepted under the perception (rightly or wrongly) that it is given with an ulterior motive, that is, to induce the exercise of public duty in a certain way.
- In the case of *extortion* a public official uses his power to force citizens to pay for the same service that they would normally be able to obtain without such payment.
- *Embezzlement* is illegal self-enrichment or simple theft by a public official without the involvement of another party.
- *Fraud* is usually the term used when an official conceals or provides misleading information on facts and figures through deceit, manipulation or distortion.

When we use the term 'corruption' here our understanding shall cover these related forms of behaviour provided that in every case the misuse of public office is involved. As gift giving is so common it is deserving of greater attention in the course of this book.

As far as types or forms of corruption are concerned, it is possible to speak of three main categories: incidental, institutional and systemic.[8]

- *Incidental* corruption covers individual acts of malfeasance such as petty (regular small payments) or grand corruption (normally involving one large payment). It could take a 'clientilist' form where a person offering a bribe obtains a higher benefit, or a 'patrimonial' one where the person receiving the bribe obtains the higher benefit. Such corruption can also be political or administrative (bureaucratic), depending on whether the corrupt person is a politician or public servant.[9]
- *Institutional* corruption is when a government department, such as the police services, is so riddled with corruption from top to bottom that corruption is a feature of most of its interactions with the public.
- A society can be defined as *systemically* corrupt when it is so infected with corruption that it becomes a fact of everyday life. Corruption is so entrenched that it is difficult to avoid and is overlooked by almost every legal authority.

If we put aside the legal norms, since these change over time and vary across countries, and since what constitutes 'illegal' is decided by someone in a public position of power, corruption can also be defined as 'behaviour which deviates from the formal rules of conduct governing the actions of someone in a position of public authority because of private-regarding motives such as wealth, power or status'.[10] With this particular approach no attempt to model the goals of power and status is made, but instead 'the economic effects of private wealth-seeking behaviour on the part of officials' become the focus for the economic analysis of corruption.[11] The main effect of corruption is understood to be 'an allocative one if as a result the final user of a resource other than the one who would have had access to the resource otherwise' benefits, while in addition, the secondary effect is that 'resources are lost in the process of corruption resulting in a decline in social output overall'.[12]

The forms of corruption are intrinsically related to their effects in multiple ways. Like an infectious disease, corruption can spread to all layers of a government-serving bureaucracy, causing untold losses of revenue and stifling public confidence in that government's ability to serve the public interest. Syndicated corruption (involving organized criminal networks) in a police department, for example, can be so widespread that it becomes difficult to perform one's duty with integrity without due consideration to a corrupt payment. A perfect case of this 'clustering effect' is when, according to Malaysian writer Sayed Hussein Alatas, 'every move from getting a letter to a file, then the file to the signatory and back again to the file and finally to the post, has to be "oiled" by bribes'.[13] Alatas also elaborates on the 'differential delivery effect' that may be observed in drug trafficking, where a dealer would pay thousands of dollars to an airport official to ignore the landing of a small plane carrying millions of dollars worth of cocaine. In this scenario, though 'the person bribed does not deliver any material good himself, the effect of his corruption is the delivery of cocaine', while the 'delivery effect is the consequence of the bribe whether it is accomplished by the recipient or not'.[14] If many similar cases of corruption were to be a feature of life in a given country, the consolidated effects would be devastating. If one's commitment to public duty is subverted in this way, corruption then becomes a way of life. But worse off are those who inhabit such a depressing world and cannot claim any benefits from the prevailing system, like a parent having her child refused university admission because she did not have the same 'connections' as others, or losing a court case because the judge was bribed. Resignation replaces outrage, and stagnation sets in as life itself becomes a victim of corruption.

Grey areas

Rents, which are earnings in excess of all relevant costs, arise when someone with a monopoly on the supply of certain goods and services charges a higher price than that which would prevail in a competitive environment. Government officials who enjoy such power may be tempted to charge 'monopoly rents' or 'speed money' as a result. The attempts to acquire them (rent-seeking) are not normally regarded as illegal or immoral if the structure of the economy or government allows for such monopolies to exist, but they often lead to corruption, if not waste and inefficiency. Thus payment of such rents may or may not be viewed as constituting corruption, depending on the context.

Lobbying should also be mentioned, as it involves decisions in the public sphere that may be put up for sale. Johann Graf Lambsdorff, a German professor, avers that since such activity is usually legal and 'carried out in a transparent and competitive manner, and involving not the narrow interests of individuals but that of larger business sectors', it should not be regarded as corruption.[15] Similarly, Yale University Scholar Susan Rose-Ackerman believes that a political system with multiple sources of authority is an effective check on corruption, as nothing can be approved unless all the bodies agree.[16] Obtaining benefits in the American political system, for instance, will be quite costly and complex, while using corrupt means to get a law passed would be equally expensive and risky. Lobbying is therefore not an activity to be frowned upon, but a commendable practice in this interpretation if citizens in a democracy are to be allowed to express their political interests by supporting political parties or electoral candidates through gifts. The issue may not be that simple, though. Robert Williams, writing in the British context, mentions that American politicians are normally expected to raise their own election funds, which makes them dependent on wealthy donors, who in return expect privileged access and strategic information.[17] Often this goes further, to the placing of obligations on public officials to intervene in administrative or legislative matters on behalf of the electoral campaign contributor. The question remains as to how one is supposed to believe that any donation made to a political party or politician is for purely altruistic or patriotic reasons and not to cement the 'bonds of reciprocity'.

Case study: Corruption and human rights

Corruption produces human rights violations and affects many lives. When individuals and families have to pay bribes to access food, housing, property, education, jobs and the right to participate in the cultural life of a community, basic human rights are clearly violated. In tackling these ills, therefore, there can be no doubt of the importance of forging closer ties between those working for human rights and those fighting against corruption. But it is also clear that to work most effectively together, the question 'Just what have human rights to do with corruption?' is one that needs further reflection. This link was highlighted for me when as High Commissioner for Human Rights, I addressed an audience of parliamentarians in Cambodia in mid-2002 on the issue of trafficking in people. The parliament was full and many eloquent speeches were made.

I then went to a village to meet representatives of a small NGO. The women had all escaped from a life of being trafficked as prostitutes and all were HIV positive. They spoke to me of corruption – of the bribery of officials and the police – and it was corruption they asked me to talk about at the press conference that was to follow. As this example shows, corruption hits the hardest at the poorest in society, those with limited or no possibilities to defend themselves. But corruption affects the whole of society as well. Decisions supposedly taken for the public good are in truth motivated by a desire for private gain and result in policies and projects that impoverish rather than enrich a country.

In order for a corrupt system to prevail, numerous other rights are likely to be restricted in the areas of political participation and access to justice. The need for the corrupt to protect themselves and their cronies undermines the electoral process, leads to intimidation and manipulation of the press and compromises the independence of the judiciary in North and South alike. Especially disturbing is the impunity that covers up so many of these acts. If human rights are violated by corruption, respect for human rights can be a powerful tool in fighting corruption.

(Extract from Mary Robinson 2004, *Corruption and Human Rights, Global Corruption Report 2004*, London: Pluto Press on behalf of Transparency International, Berlin, p. 7.)

Illegal but not corrupt behaviour

It is important, as Lambsdorff says, to distinguish corruption from other forms of criminal conduct that do not involve the misuse of public office.[18] These would include cases of tax evasion, insider dealings on the stock market, production of counterfeit money, subsidy fraud, and contraband, all of which are excluded from our focus.

The benefits of 'fighting' corruption

Economic analyses of corruption have often been used, as we shall later see, to determine the *benefits* that corruption can bring to a developing society. This is not a question to which we shall pay too much attention as it has been shown that 'cases in which corruption enhances the efficiency of agents and improves the allocation of public services are limited', something Susan Rose-Ackerman has made clear, and that '[t]he theoretical and empirical evidence does not support widespread tolerance of corruption'.[19] While some economic models are useful in calculating the costs of fighting corruption, little would be achieved if we were to advance possible arguments about the benefit value of corruption.

Those who write about corruption are mostly inclined toward establishing the costs of corruption, which usually have a negative impact on a country and its peoples. Our concern, on the other hand, is with the investment that society must make in the effort to overcome corruption, aspects of which can be measured in monetary terms and which will usually have implications for a country's resources. If a country's national treasury keeps public money in trust, on behalf of its citizens, and uses such money to procure public benefits, by obtaining goods and services, costs will arise. Citizens will receive and experience value for the money spent on their behalf that can be viewed as benefits, that is, if what is done on their behalf is effective. Costs in the public sphere can include opportunity costs (i.e. the value of the best alternative that one forfeits by making a specific choice), actual costs (recorded or incurred expenses, as opposed to those anticipated or forecast), maintenance costs (typically the costs for labour and parts to repair anything), and social costs (the total costs of any action). Our concern is with the monetary costs insofar as an appropriation is made or not made from a national budget to fight corruption. An increase in costs on a certain budget item is usually justified in terms of the added benefits that are supposed to accrue from the increased investment cost. We shall therefore be concerned to understand what the nature, quality and quantity of benefits will be if the costs of fighting corruption are increased.

The origin of the term 'fighting' corruption is obscure. It has come into common usage from the 1990s onwards with the rise of civil society movements against corruption like Transparency International, a not-for-profit, non-governmental organization (NGO) formed in 1993 to curb corruption. Its origin may possibly be linked to the fight against corruption in Hong Kong in the 1970s. It has come to signify the attempt to eradicate corruption (as far as this is possible) from society by the joint efforts of government, civil society, the private sector, the media and the international community. 'Fighting corruption' is often used interchangeably with 'combating' or 'curbing' corruption, while 'preventing' corruption has longer-term connotations. One can act to prevent corruption from occurring at all, and one can act after corruption has already taken place (combat). 'Controlling' corruption is a preferred term for some, rather than fighting, though it would denote the same act or actions to bring about a reduction in corruption. The term 'controlling corruption' seems to assume that while governments may take action against corruption, it will not be eradicated. 'Fighting corruption' is increasingly being used as the preferred term by governments around the world, presumably because of the stronger intent which it may convey about the political will to be intolerant of any form of corruption and to communicate such intolerance to the public (or voters).

Corruption hotspots

If it has proved difficult to provide a fully comprehensive definition of corruption, it is equally challenging to tabulate all probable factors that give rise to its practice. Still, it is worth looking at some attempts that have been made to understand the contextual factors that cause corruption to flourish.

Africa

According to John Mbaku, the African context provides one with a pattern of recurring circumstances that in one way or another seems to invite opportunistic and corrupt behaviour. The first such circumstance is the presence of the 'soft state' across the continent, where citizens have a low sense of national interest and a diffuse sense of commitment to public service.[20] Civil servants in many countries see public service 'as an opportunity to generate wealth for themselves, their families and their friends' and can themselves be extremely inefficient and incompetent.[21] A country's prospects of economic growth and development can be severely retarded by such incompetence, inefficiency and unprofessional behaviour. Increased levels of poverty and unequal distribution of income are further contributory factors that slow growth. The cultural 'ethic' often requires that civic virtue be set aside in favour of a higher obligation to one's family or friends. All these factors combine to make Africa a breeding ground for the proliferation of corrupt practices.[22]

The African experience of corruption, however, cannot be explained without reference to the role of colonialism. According to

Robert Williams, 'the kinds of bureaucracies which developed in most African states provided classic breeding grounds for what might be called the politics of envy'.[23] The life of the ordinary peasant offered a stark contrast to that of the civil servant bureaucrat, with the one enjoying access to education, recruitment and advancement within the colonial system and the other condemned to a life of poverty. These disparities in lifestyle and incomes were merely confirmed after independence, when priority shifted to Africanization of the civil service, which also meant expanding the bureaucracy. Colonialism served to profoundly alter 'the structure and scale of incentives, opportunities and rewards'.[24] Williams is also emphatic that, 'if corruption involves, in part, bribery and buying the co-operation of those in authority, it was employed from the earliest days of colonial expansion to secure the collaboration of traditional rulers'.[25] If public duty and personal service were denigrated during the colonial era, it was no different thereafter as new African leaders often saw the business of government as giving direction from the top rather than leading from below through citizen participation. Status, power and influence were enjoyed, where the local village mattered more than the national interest. The new African states were after all colonial creations with artificial boundaries and it is difficult to imagine a shared sense of identity and belonging, and of loyalty to the state. The public interest would have been an abstract and meaningless notion to people who experienced government as distant and impersonal. Their resolve to bring about change, often in the face of failure, would include attempts to use corrupt methods of holding government more responsible for attending to their needs. If the colonial factor in encouraging the spread of corruption is established, though, it is not easy to find evidence that post-colonial Africa has been any less corrupt.[26]

Asia

In the Asian context, the cultural factor is again a key determinant in understanding the prevalence of corruption. In India, for example, a normative pattern may be observed where 'greater importance is given to duty than to law. Duty is interpreted as duty to family, oneself and one's own community. Law is then interpreted as subordinate to duty and relationships as more important than rules [and] may be bent to serve relationships'.[27] The legal system is thus undermined by a higher authority and is often therefore resisted.

Case study: Corruption in Iraq

The International Advisory Board for Iraq (IAMB), the independent oversight body that holds the proceeds of oil export sales from Iraq, surplus funds from the Oil-for-Food Programme, and Iraqi assets frozen abroad found several indicators for misuse of funds over oil extraction by the Coalition Provisional Authority (CPA) that initially took over running Iraq after the US-led invasion. The CPA was responsible for the absence of oil-metering, inadequate record keeping, uneven application of contracting procedures, insufficient payroll records, deviation from tendering procedures, and inadequate contract monitoring. In thirteen months, the Coalition Provisional Authority disbursed or obligated US$19.6 billion in contracts, more than 90% of the Development Fund for Iraq then available. This money belonged to the Iraqi people as it was money derived from the sales of Iraqi oil.

One audit determined that the coalition government could not account for almost US$9 billion from the Development Fund for Iraq. However, hearings of the US Congress House Government Oversight Committee formed the view that US$12 billion went missing and no paper trail exists to explain what happened to it, a view the former head of the CPA, Paul Bremer, did not dispute. The US$12 billion represents about a third of the Iraq reconstruction budget for 2003. At least US$1 billion on money from the Development Fund for Iraq (DFI) disappeared in dubious military contracts. Ali Allawi, Iraq's finance minister, complained that these contracts were awarded without bidding and the money was paid up front with great speed out of the ministry's account.

(Extract from Bessy Andriotis and Cath James (eds) 2008, *From Corruption to Good Governance*, Uniting Church in Australia, Synod of Victoria and Tasmania, p. 53.)

Developing countries

These cultural arguments should not detract from the basic premise that any human being is subject to temptation in any walk or station of life and corruption can arise as a defect of human nature. There are also those in developing countries who believe that it has less to do with their behaviour than with that of those in the developed world who initiate and export production of goods, services and bad practices.[28] Hence the notion that the major part of the problem of corruption sits in the developing world is one that is highly contested. The cause of corruption has also been ascribed to the fact that people are often placed in compromising situations of having to choose the lesser of two evils (for example, self-enrichment over against adding to the coffers of a military dictator), or to use immoral means to justify moral ends.

The public sector

The public sector in the developed world has expanded enormously over the past century and has been largely penetrated by market values. Politicians are often required to decide on contracts for massive public works and welfare programmes involving large sums of money, while the same politicians belong to parties that must run costly campaigns to ensure their re-election. Corporate political funding then becomes competitive where 'buying voters, legislators and state officials is "good business" if it produces cost-effective results'.[29] When the boundaries of capitalism and democracy can be merged to achieve such self-serving ends, the reconfiguration of the public and private domains of power gives rise to its unchecked usage for corrupt purposes. The basic misfit between the two systems (political and economic) causes the majority will of citizens to come up against the narrow interests of economic power. Politicians would ordinarily be the mediators in cases of competing interests between the two in a democracy but, as John Girling points out, 'prudent politicians cannot afford seriously to jeopardize business interests, because in the long term an effective economy is crucial to political survival'.[30] For this reason also, even politicians of high integrity are often tempted to compromise on justice and the rule of law for the private benefit of a few corporate elites. This collusion (the accommodation between politics and economics) is then the precondition for corruption to occur. Yet given that corruption can thus be attributed to a whole range of possibilities, as is mostly the case, it becomes very difficult to attempt more than a cursory discussion of the contextual factors that give rise to its origin at any given time.

Measuring corruption

The extent of a problem such as corruption must first be known (usually through instruments of measurement) before one attempts to find its solution (usually involving an application of resources).

Calculating the costs of ways to manage the impact of corruption will require some prior knowledge of the nature and degree of such impact. In a twist of irony, one observer wrote that 'if corruption could be measured, it could probably be eliminated'.[31] Counting only the number of bribes paid would ignore the number of corrupt acts that accompany such payments. To measure the occurrence of such acts would require that they be reported. Corruption by its very nature is not a transparent activity and so scientific information or simple data about its prevalence cannot be reliably procured. Statistics compiled on the basis of questionnaires may be viewed with suspicion if they are seen to be biased towards rumours instead of direct observation. Yet this has not dampened the spirits of some who have tried, at least indirectly, to obtain information about the extent of corruption in a country or institution. Paolo Mauro was probably the first to bring corruption into the field of economic growth studies when he measured the effects of corruption on a country's growth rate.[32] The results showed a significant negative impact and there is now a strong consensus among many economists that corruption retards economic growth.

The Corruption Perceptions Index

One of the earliest tools to measure corruption was devised by Lambsdorff. Despite his acceptance that 'quantitative estimates of the extent of corruption are usually difficult to provide', and that objective data is probably irretrievable, he nevertheless negotiates what in his view is a 'plausible approach' out of this impasse.[33] He produces, annually for Transparency International, the Corruption Perceptions Index (CPI) by rating countries according to the subjective perceptions of informed observers. These are normally business people, political analysts and foreign-aid workers. Perceptions of course do not equate to reality, but since the CPI is a composite index, relying on 15 data sources from institutions like the World Bank, it can be used as a useful measure of cross-country corruption, particularly as the perceptions tend to correlate among the various observers. (The full CPI is shown in the Appendix on pp. 147–51 and gives a list of countries from, according to the CPI, the least corrupt to the most corrupt.)

Because our knowledge of corruption is so 'incomplete and limited', a survey among 'experts in the field' was carried out by Dutch scholar Leo Huberts in 1996 to determine just how serious a problem corruption was. His method involved sending a question-naire to participants from three international anti-corruption and ethics conferences and aggregating their responses with the views of another smaller panel of experts. Huberts concluded that corruption 'might have more in common in different geographical and cultural contexts' and suggested the need for comparative case studies to confirm whether the findings of his research would differ from 'actual corruption and fraud practices'.[34]

Alternatives to the CPI

One of the more recent ways of providing a 'quantitative scorecard of governance practices' in 25 selected countries includes the attempt to measure not corruption but its opposite, namely 'the extent of citi-zens' ability to ensure their government is open and accountable'.[35] The existence of laws and institutions, their effectiveness and public access to information is the focus of this 'Public Integrity Index' that is compiled by the Centre for Public Integrity, an NGO based in Washington DC and whose mission is to put relevant information into the public domain so that public officials can be held to greater levels of accountability. Countries with a 'strong' ranking on this index, like South Africa, Germany, Australia and the United States, are viewed as being globally competitive in having the requisite laws and institutions in place to deter corruption.[36]

Although the CPI remains the most widely used measure of those mentioned above, it is not without its problems. It is unclear whether what is being measured involves the frequency of corrupt activities or the actual amounts of money being paid as bribes, or both. Countries of the developing world take exception to being placed at the lower end of the CPI, thus indicating their high vulner-ability to corruption, which in turn deters their investment poten-tial. Partly in response to this complaint, a Bribe Payers Index (BPI) was also launched in 1999 by Transparency International to measure the propensity of firms from industrialized countries to win contracts by paying bribes abroad.

The country listed last on the CPI is inevitably perceived to be the most corrupt in the world, but since not all countries are listed, such a conclusion should not be drawn. Believing that a more explicit and comprehensive tool was needed, World Bank researchers embarked on an ambitious project of estimating six dimensions of governance in 199 countries and territories from 1996 to 2002.[37] Several hundred individual indicators of governance perception from 25 different sources were used. Country coverage was obviously expanded but, as the researchers acknowledge, margins of error remain, and these must be considered when countries are compared with one another and over time.

The role of the churches in fighting corruption

If corruption amounts to a misuse of public office for private gain, and if it has manifested itself in unmanageable ways in the developing world over the past two or three decades, such that it has prompted Western scholars to devise tools for its measurement, has it ever caught the attention of any faith community? One participant at a church-sponsored conference on corruption, a European business executive working in the area of risk management, remarked that in his ten years' experience of attending anti-corruption conferences he had not encountered a church leader. In his words, 'It is essential that the churches be an active voice in national discussions.'[38] At the 8th Assembly of the World Council of Churches (WCC) in Harare, Zimbabwe, held in December 1998, a most forthright statement was made by Protestant churches about corruption, albeit in the context of the struggle to provide debt relief to developing nations. Representatives of over 350 million Christians called on their member churches to advocate for 'ethical governance in all countries' and urged governments to take 'legislative action against all forms of corruption and misuse of loans'.[39] Delegates at the assembly furthermore, in the debate on human rights, recognized that 'corrupt practices are a major evil in our societies' and pledged therefore to uphold the 'elementary right' of every person to be protected under the law against such practices. As the threat of corruption to development was not being viewed comprehensively enough, at least at this time, nothing of substance has emanated from the WCC since. At its subsequent assembly held in Porto Alegre, Brazil, in February 2005, despite the full onslaught of global capital on poorer nations, and the rapid rise of corrupt practices throughout the world, nothing new was mentioned about the evolving fight against corruption. The WCC's reluctance to speak out against corruption might be viewed as a missed opportunity for prophetic engagement when the 'signs of the times' were everywhere present. Yet other churches elsewhere, especially those in Latin America, have not been silent in the face of the new pervasive evil.

Fresh from having lived through periods of undemocratic rule, military dictatorships and authoritarian regimes, countries in Latin America have begun to experience a new wave of democratic participation in civic life. From Brazil to Bolivia, from Chile to Paraguay, and from Nicaragua to Costa Rica, civil society movements have spawned a new and vibrant experience of participatory democracy, one where the churches have been no silent witnesses. On the contrary, in the words of one missionary observer, 'very large numbers of Christians filled the ranks of human rights groups formerly against military abuses and now against corruption'.[40] Many of these would be members of small Christian communities while others were leaders of churches, like Cardinal Oscar Rodriguez, the Archbishop of Tegucigalpa in Honduras. He rose to prominence when, almost by default, he was invited to lead a national commission against corruption and also went on to become President of the Latin American Bishops' Conference from 1995 to 1999. Using this latter platform, the Cardinal helped lay a solid foundation for making corruption 'the new battle horse of the Catholic Church' in Latin America. In the Philippines, another part of the world dominated by Catholic Christians, church leaders have adopted 'people power' campaigns to oust corrupt leaders. Archbishop Angel Lagdameo, President of the Catholic Bishops' Conference there, has pleaded for a revolt against endemic corruption perpetrated by President Gloria Arroyo, who faced mounting calls to resign amid bribery allegations against her government.

From the most cursory reading of church history it should be apparent that churches have not completely ignored the prevalence and practice of corruption in society. John Wesley spoke out against it in his time and at the 1767 Methodist Conference he asked delegates to ponder the question of how bribery could be prevented at the ensuing elections.[41] We can safely assume that the 'Christian faith and tradition has a long history of condemning corruption' but this has not been clearly and unequivocally apparent.[42] Throughout their history, Christian churches have played a dubious role in facilitating corrupt practices within their own ranks and outright condemnation has been slow in coming, if at all. Consider the abuse of trust and power by parish priests for personal, or sometimes sexual gratification, and the fact that many such known cases remain un-punished. If we had to imagine the number of times when the noble values of transparency and accountability, so necessary in the fight against corruption, have been trampled upon in the name of the-ocracy we will hesitate to paint the churches as acting virtuously in these matters. The churches' complicity in corrupt behaviour is not, however, the primary concern of this book.

The challenge to fight the abuse of public office for private gain is still not something the churches should be afraid of adopting. The struggle for the moral transformation of society does not require that artisans for the new humanity in Christ be first themselves 'cleansed' from corrupt influences, as though this is ever possible. Churches have brought and can bring their moral capital, accumu-lated over centuries and embracing the entire world, to bear on the global effort to combat and prevent corruption. A much more nuanced, thorough and contemporary understanding of the problem and its current manifestations is a prerequisite if we are to be effect-ive in adding strategic value to efforts already under way. As the Vatican so wisely recognized when the fight against corruption be-came a subject for reflection within its precincts, we should initially aim 'to arrive at a better understanding of the phenomenon of cor-ruption' before we attempt to devise ways of contributing towards its reduction in society.[43]

2

When and why corruption happens

Researching corruption

Corruption as a matter of scientific inquiry is a relatively new development. By 1957 *The Economist* found it 'curious' that so little attention was being given to 'one of the most obvious gaps in general textbooks on economics or political science', that of what it termed the 'unwritten section on graft'.[1] This observation had been confirmed a year earlier by Eric McKitrick of the University of Chicago, who noted that the analytical investigation of corruption 'does not seem to present a subject of very intense interest to social scientists these days'.[2] Nearly a decade later, Colin Leys of the University of Sussex in England was complaining that 'no general study in English has appeared' and that the 'systematic investigation of corruption is overdue'.[3] Gunnar Myrdal wrote from a South Asian perspective that 'it is almost taboo as a research topic and is rarely mentioned in scholarly discussions' owing to what he termed 'diplomacy in research', although corruption was an issue often raised in public debate.[4] He proceeded forthwith to break the taboo, as the lack of investigation was not related to any difficulty with the lack of an empirical method for corruption research. Numerous other studies began to appear, mostly in scholarly journals, as the reigning paucity began to give way.[5] The approaches that were regnant during the 1960s, though, were never fully developed, owing to the lack of adequate data, and academic interest waned as a result.

The advent of the 1970s saw the rise of neo-Marxist approaches to the development debate as the issue of corruption remained largely neglected. If corruption was acknowledged, it was inevitably as a 'by-product of capitalist democracy and an intrinsically corrupt international capitalist system in which lower class groups are routinely and systematically exploited'.[6] When such analyses began to decline in the 1980s as rhetoric was contradicted by observed patterns of living in socialist states, the situation changed again as the

study of corruption received fresh impetus. Still, it merited a quali-
fication like that by the world-renowned Robert Klitgaard: 'The first
thing that needs to be said is that corruption is a sensitive subject.'[7]
This was also a time when 'any mention of bribery and corruption
at international meetings would have been brushed aside' as it was
viewed to be 'too value laden, too culture bound, too vague to be the
subject of international debate'.[8] Others, like Susan Rose-Ackerman,
believed that a confrontation was needed with the basic fundamentals of political economy in modern society; she had already begun
the first of her elaborate works on corruption in the late 1970s.[9]

By the 1990s, however, the situation changed dramatically. The
study of corruption had created a 'virtual explosion' and spawned a
'growth industry', especially with economists from universities and
financial institutions now analysing its causes and effects. Even more,
it was now no longer being viewed as a phenomenon confined to
developing countries, but was seen as incidentally present in liberal
Western democratic systems of government as well. Some of the
current research challenges in fact include the extent to which democratic institutions themselves, such as a traditional political party,
might actually serve to stimulate corrupt practices.

A turning point was possibly the formation of Transparency
International in 1993 as a new civil society coalition against corruption. This was followed by the president of the World Bank who, in
1996, firmly placed corruption at centre stage as an issue of ongoing
challenge for economic development. Instead of the 'apathy, cynicism,
and denial' of the past, the World Bank, International Monetary Fund
(IMF) and other international organizations were by 1998 'seeking
to curb bribery and other corrupt practices'.[10] No longer then would
concerns about governance and corruption be diplomatically or aca-
demically isolated as the impinging reality of globalization, the end
of the Cold War, and arrival of new technologies, notably the internet, ushered in new ways of thinking, understanding and living. The
economic transformation of the states of the former Soviet Union,
increased awareness of the negative impact and monetary costs of
corruption, and the availability of numerous indicators devised from
empirical studies have further caused the flood of writings to continue unabated.[11] Some of these more recent studies have given
greater attention to issues of prevention and control of corruption
and will therefore be discussed later in terms of their relevance to
developing a national strategy of fighting corruption.

Major theories regarding corruption

Against the above background it is now possible to identify some of the most important theories and models that have been put forward to explain why corruption occurs in some situations and not others. We shall look at authors who often characterize the time in which they wrote, outlining the nature of their arguments and assessing the impact of their contributions. We begin with what might be termed the 'moralistic' approach, where corruption is recognized a priori as a human or social evil with no attendant benefits. Next we tackle the cultural approach, in which corruption arises in the context of gift giving. Then follows a discussion of the functionalist or revisionist approach – popular in the 1960s and still fascinating to some – which argued that corruption actually serves society. We shall also consider the principal-agent-client theory which rose to prominence in the 1970s, and the public choice model, which attempts to suggest ways and means of curbing corruption. Finally, some economic modifications of the functionalist model, which arose mostly in the South East Asian context of phenomenal economic growth, are examined.

A moralistic approach

As mentioned at the start of this chapter, corruption as a subject of academic discourse has not featured prominently until recent years. Yet whenever it has been under scrutiny, there have always been advocates of a moralizing approach who have added to the debate from either a religious, behaviourist, communist or imperialist perspective. In each case the basis whereby corruption was found to be anathema to society rested on an a priori approach that was value driven and not immediately related to cause and effect. For example, writing in the *African Communist*, Toussaint claimed that communist leaders earn their reputation 'through selflessness and incorruptibility in the period when they neither hold power nor stand on the threshold of power' and that socialist experiences of corruption are 'seldom driven by the pursuit of personal riches'.[12] While somewhat extreme, such a view is not contrary to what many Marxist and neo-Marxist scholars would have argued to be the inherent merits of socialism over against the flagrant distortions of capitalism. The absence of studies on corruption growing or arising from within socialist countries by such scholars is further evidence of their tacit acceptance of such rhetoric.

A greater silence on the subject of corruption is that exhibited by the theological fraternity over the past century. While the biblical injunction against bribery and corrupt practices might have been acknowledged, there has been no sustained engagement with the issue in any ecclesial tradition. Sin, of course, has been the preoccupation of the Christian Church from its origins, but the elaborate essays on the subject would usually cover matters of sexual conduct. As one American judge concluded in his magisterial study on bribes, 'It was as though at a certain level of theological sophistication or at a certain level of class consciousness it was agreed that everyone knew what constituted bribery, that everyone knew that bribery was wrong, and that no problems existed worthy of debate or discussion.'[13] This should not imply that space and time were not made for the condemnation of corrupt behaviour, however, as we saw earlier. The Ghanaian Catholic Bishops' Conference has over time called on institutions to 'crusade against bribery and corruption first from within and then fan outwards towards secular society', while in 1994 the larger African Synod of Bishops blamed greedy African politicians for having embezzled public funds.[14] The presence of moral indignation in the absence of academic engagement in the religious domain can be seen as symptomatic of a moralizing approach that may be traced to ideological dispositions as well, as we shall see next.

In explaining the prevalence of corruption in developing countries, particularly the new states of West Africa, Ronald Wraith and Edgar Simpkins were emphatic that corruption had 'nothing to with traditional values, with the African personality, or with the adaptation to Western values', but everything to do with pure avarice: 'the wrong that is done is done in the full knowledge that it is wrong, for the concept of theft does not vary as between Christian and Muslim, African and European'.[15] This approach might also underlie the methodology of measuring corruption in the sense that the occurrence as such is bad, irrespective of the consequences. Furthermore, as Leys has shown, these writers 'conceive of the problem as one of seeking in British history the causes which led to the triumph in Britain of this point of view, with its attendant advantages, in the hope that African and other developing countries might profit from the experience of Britain'.[16] The fundamental problem with this approach is one of comparative morality, where one set of values relative to one country is regarded as superior to others. Wraith and Simpkins were obviously referring to the cultural pressures common in African societies where rights of individuals were superseded by those of the extended family, and where duty took precedence over laws. Civil servants might be expected to share the benefits of their positions with members of their immediate family and ethnic group, as such an obligation was culturally accepted. Corruption may therefore involve an ostensibly immoral act with strong normative undertones. This is a matter to which we must turn next.

A cultural approach

In the African tradition, and in many other cultures as well, leaders were expected to be kind and compassionate towards their people, especially in times of sickness or distress. Thus, for example, public officials would be held responsible for making 'decisions based on personal and not impersonal norms'.[17] Africans might even end up condemning corruption when it did not benefit them personally or their relatives, and might condone it when it brought them some benefits. John Mbaku has also drawn attention to the African practice where young men and women, upon migrating to urban areas in search of employment, would rely on their more established relatives there to provide food and shelter in their new surroundings.[18] Even more, if one such relative held a senior civil service position, he or she would be expected to provide job security as well. Such age-old cultural expectations can so easily nurture the practice of corruption in a new political environment, as Monday Ekpo has also shown. He writes that the Nigerian traditional practice of gift giving is 'not merely a mechanism of manipulation and influence' but 'is embedded in a network of social alliances and status differences'.[19] Thus gift giving is essentially 'a self-perpetuating system of belief and action grounded in the society's value system' and explains the prevalence of bureaucratic corruption in Nigeria to a large extent.[20] One's culture establishes bonds of reciprocity between people that are then held sacred for all times.

Of course the above cultural dynamic has often degenerated into extreme forms of neo-patrimonialism (a form of government based on the rule by family households, usually patriarchal) where kleptocracy, personal rule and 'prebendalism'[21] have resulted. Its core features include 'personal relationships as the foundation of the political system, clientelism (sometimes also nepotism), presidentialism (political monopolization), and a very weak distinction between public and private'.[22] Yet it remains important for any act of corruption to be understood 'with reference to the social relationships between people in historically specific settings. A transaction is now a legal one, now illegal, depending on its social context.'[23] Legal frameworks assume that corruption involves an objective act committed within neatly defined parameters and this is mostly not the case. Corruption in Africa, it seems, was fuelled because administrative machinery imported entirely from Europe was expected to produce similar outcomes while scant attention was given to the possibility of conflicting norms.[24] Often the colonial legacy of inefficiency, authoritarianism, strong centralized bureaucracy and poor service delivery was merely transposed into the normative framework of the new public services. Britain is thus blamed for contributing to corruption in colonial Africa by allowing a situation to develop where 'power was given to those who clamoured for it most, with the consequence that few well-trained administrators and officers, whose indoctrination with the impersonal bureaucratic virtues had made some progress, were surrounded by half-baked newcomers, and became subordinated to the politicians who had reached the top by demagoguery and huckstering'.[25] The distrust, frustration, dishonesty and complacency of one bureaucratic system were merely replaced by another whose officials knew no better. Corruption can therefore be seen as the result of a clash of cultures, a cost which society must bear in order to advance.

Case study: Kenyan football corruption

The outside world associates Kenyan sporting prowess with the rigours of medium and long-distance running, but football (soccer) is the country's favourite domestic sport, with a fan base of at least ten million. But Kenyan football has been plagued for decades by ethnic antagonism and political intrigue. Now, it has become clear that the game is also a hotbed of fraud and corruption. An initiative by concerned football clubs, in partnership with Transparency International-Kenya, is seeking to give the game a new sort of 'fix' by tackling these problems.

Widespread mismanagement of the game in the office of its organising body, the Kenyan Football Federation (KFF), has long been apparent. Gross incompetence and likely bribery of referees is all too common, and the embezzlement of KFF funds has also come to light. The KFF has not sent audited accounts to its member clubs for decades. In some KFF clubs and national teams, players and coaches go unpaid for months on end. Overloaded match schedules, arbitrary changes in the appointment of match officials, the abuse of rules and manipulation in the promotion and relegation of teams regularly disappoint fans.

Eight Premier League clubs came together in December 2000 to create the Inter-Club Consultative Group (ICCG) to petition the KFF over these trends. The ICCG protest subsequently unravelled a complex of financial intrigue in spite of KFF resistance.

A copy of the KFF audit for 2000 was leaked, revealing major irregularities in the Federation's book-keeping. Only US$26,923 (= 2.1 million Kenyan shillings) was recorded for gate collections during 2000, although the year witnessed over 300 league, cup and international matches. Meanwhile, stadium expenses tripled from US$10,066 to over US$29,487 in 2000, although 150 fewer matches were played that year. Official allowances and 'youth expenses' similarly rose massively, but inexplicably, during the same period.

In response to these alarming findings, the ICCG sent a letter to the KFF Secretary General in May 2001, asking the KFF to call a meeting of all clubs to discuss the audit issue and general levels of accountability. The letter was returned unopened with an annotation stating: 'Mail back. We do not know this group since they are not our members.' Direct appeals to the Confederation of African Football (CAF) and the International Federation of Football Associations (FIFA) also fell on deaf ears.

(Extract from *Global Corruption Report 2001*, Berlin: Transparency International, 2001, p. 76.)

A functional approach

The functionalist approach (also known as the revisionist or structuralist approach) extends the cultural approach to argue that corruption serves a useful function in society: it has positive effects and redeeming qualities over against its costs during periods of national development. Robert Merton provides a theoretical framework for this approach when he analyses the 'structural context' of American city politics in the 1900s and traces the rise of alternative 'Mafia' styled sources of authority within the urban context.[26] First, he shows how agents of the city machine would provide a humane and personal service in response to claims of assistance for all and sundry by bypassing cold bureaucratic procedures in return for votes. Second, the 'boss' served to grease the wheels of business by providing safe passage and protection through the unfriendly regulatory and unrestricted competitive environments. The third function of this alternative power base was to serve as a medium to achieve social mobility, particularly for new immigrants or minority ethnic groups who sought to ingratiate themselves among the established elites in their quest for money and success. Lastly, the racketeer of illegitimate business was also able (in return for kickbacks, of course) to 'fix things when necessary with appropriate government officials' and, like the legitimate businessman, strive to meet market demand and maximize his gains in the sale of goods and services.[27] If all of the above constituted corruption, it still appears to have been able to improve the 'administrative capacity of governments, encourage entrepreneurship, thereby promoting economic growth and, by incorporating the disaffected and the poor, foster social integration'.[28]

In a related functionalist mode, if corruption is about buying favours from bureaucrats responsible for a government's economic policy in the interests of administrative flexibility, it can be extremely useful, according to Nathaniel Leff.[29] Economic development is made possible by a higher rate of investment which requires a minimum risk of uncertainty. Corruption arises as a form of insurance, guaranteeing expected outcomes but also directing economic activity when governments pursue the wrong policies. It can also promote competition and efficiency by providing quick access to scarcities like import permits, foreign exchange and government contracts. Corruption can even enable an economic innovator to introduce his product or service before he has had time to establish his political credentials. Governments of underdeveloped countries, says Leff, should not be assumed to have as their goal the promotion of economic policies that are beneficial to the global market. But he belies his neo-colonial outlook by dubiously assuming, on the other hand, that developed countries would normally pursue sound economic policies for sustainable development amid low levels of corruption.

Samuel Huntington, a famous American professor, similarly viewed corruption that is caused by the expansion of government regulations as having a stimulating effect on economic growth. In his words, it 'may be one way of surmounting traditional laws or bureaucratic regulations which hamper economic expansion' and can at times 'contribute to political development by helping to strengthen political parties'.[30] Corruption is again the 'lubricant' that overcomes red tape and should be seen as 'a product of modernization' if countries are to progress in their political consciousness. The moral implication here is that economic benefits are viewed as the highest good. More recently, Osterfeld has argued for the advantageous role that 'expansive corruption' can play in improving economic development by removing bottlenecks from the bureaucracy and making it more responsive to entrepreneurial needs.[31] In his scheme bribery can also serve to accelerate the participation of the citizenry in national development. Yet, as Ekpo observed in the Nigerian context for instance, functionalist views of the positive benefits of corruption have little or no value because of their 'myopic selectivity' and 'empirical irrelevance'.[32] Morocco, with a monarchical regime, has also been used to show that corruption actually helps maintain bureaucratic inefficiency instead of removing it and contributes to the development of a privileged class of bureaucrats at odds with the masses.[33] Furthermore, the relevance of the functionalist approach for the United States is questionable as 'a majority of the evidence seems to be against its application' there.[34]

The principal-agent-client model

One of the first uses of the principal-agent-client conceptual scheme was that by Edward Banfield in an exploratory paper he published in 1975.[35] In his quest to identify the major variables of corruption in governmental agencies of the United States, he used the following frame of reference involving the principal and his agent to describe the classic corruption scenario in a bureaucracy:

> The agent is the person who has accepted an obligation (as in an employment contract) to act on behalf of his principal in some range of matters and, in doing so, to serve the principal's interest as if it were his own. The principal may be a person or an entity such as an organization or public. In acting on behalf of his principal an agent must exercise some 'discretion'; the wider the range (measured in terms of the principal's interest) among which he may choose, the broader is his discretion. The situation includes 'clients' – 'third parties', either persons or abstract entities – who stand to lose or gain by the action of the agent.[36]

Banfield also mentions the presence of 'rules' as a contingency factor that may or may not involve sanctions and penalties and which may or may not be enforced. He is convinced that it is easier for private firms to exercise restraint on employees guilty of corruption than it is for a government that is inhibited by civil service regulations.[37] Banfield's assumption, of course, is that more rules create more opportunities for bypassing them, hence more corruption and more calls for deregulation. More rules also make it more difficult to dismiss someone guilty of corruption. While recognizing the deterrent effects of monitoring and unfavourable publicity upon corrupt behaviour, though, he seems to view any extension of governmental authority as necessarily facilitating the spread of corruption.

Following Banfield, Susan Rose-Ackerman found the standard approaches of political science to corruption to be inadequate and attempted to develop a more political and economic theory of corruption. She started with the premise that the 'delegation of decision-making authority is a fundamental organizational technique. Whenever an agent is given discretionary authority, corruption provides a way for the objectives of higher authority to be undermined.'[38] The principal-agent-client relationship therefore becomes her unit of analysis as her concern embraces all payments made to agents that are not passed on to the principal. Moral costs in illegal transactions are also mentioned, as 'the importance of personal honesty and a devotion to democratic ideals' are viewed as critical to effective representative government.[39] Use of this model, as Robert Klitgaard has observed, opens up several possibilities where 'Illicit activities will be greater when agents have monopoly power over clients, agents enjoy discretion, and accountability is poor. Clients will be most willing to pay bribes when they reap monopoly rents from the service provided by the agents.'[40] The honest principal at the top of the hierarchy, as is the usual assumption, has meanwhile to 'analyse the extent of the various kinds of corruption, assess their costs and possible benefits, and then undertake (costly) corrective measures up to the point where the marginal benefits in terms of reduced corruption match the marginal costs of the corrective measures'.[41] By this token, the optimal level of corruption is therefore not zero in as much as the maximum level of anti-corruption effort is not equal to infinity. The now hackneyed term 'zero tolerance', often used by politicians to signal political intent to fight corruption, therefore becomes meaningless.

A variant on the principal-agent-client model, known as incentive theory, describes the situation when the goals of both employer and employee are aligned. It has been used in the case of modern Russia to show, contrary to the functionalist approach discussed above, that corruption can be costly to economic development. In the presence of a weak centralized government, foreign investors shy away in the face of a deluge of bribery demands from a host of bureaucracies competing for 'territoriality'.[42] However, if agents are allowed to compete in the provision of the same services, the likelihood of corruption will be reduced if such agents cannot simply steal. This approach has provided a conceptual framework for many other scholars seeking to analyse the role that public officials can play in reshaping the bureaucracy with incentive schemes and disciplinary measures that may ultimately lead to reduced corruption.[43] These include changes in the system of rewards (especially higher wages) and penalties, and in the process of selecting agents, information gathering, and the restructuring of the principal-client-agent relationship itself. Such changes are closely related, of course, to the main problem which the principal has in this model, namely, different objectives from those of the agent and lack of information about the agent's character and activities. In a tax bureau, for example, such a disadvantage can have a substantive and spiralling effect. State coffers will be robbed of needed revenue if agents' illicit behaviour is not kept in check, where such behaviour will either have an infectious impact on these agents' colleagues in a centralized bureaucracy or serve to lower morale among other, more diligent colleagues. Another limitation to the application of this approach is that it does not explain why, in situations with similar wage incentives and monitoring mechanisms, corruption levels vary (as between two municipal tax bureaux in the same state). Neither does it offer clues as to why agents behave in noble ways even when the possibility of detection is low.[44] Wage incentives are nonetheless a factor that may have to be borne in mind in determining one's approach to fighting corruption among public officials.

Public choice theory

The public choice model uses the techniques of economics to understand what governments actually do rather than recommend what they should do.[45] Here marketplace behaviour is always viewed by economists as being motivated by private interests, while politicians are believed to behave according to their own definition of the public interest. Separate understandings have evolved to explain human behaviour: a self-interested individual seeking personal benefits over against a public actor intent on maximizing societal welfare.[46] From the public choice perspective, however, private interest pressures are seen as central to the process of policy formulation, and no longer simply as an obstacle to the adoption of better policies. The fundamental premise of public choice theory is that all individuals involved in the policy process, especially politicians and bureaucrats, are seen as 'rational actors attempting to improve their own welfare, rather than some abstract notion of social welfare'.[47] All political actors seek to maximize their personal benefits in politics as well as in the marketplace – voters, taxpayers, interest groups, bureaucrats, and so forth. Government arises as a form of 'social contract' among individuals who agree to obey laws for their mutual benefit and support the state in exchange for protection of their own lives, liberty and property.[48] Politicians are less interested in advancing principles than in winning elections, and will for this reason fail to offer clear policy alternatives in election campaigns. In the public choice school of thought, the 'natural tendencies' of politicians and bureaucrats are to expand their power base in society, and they will, as a result, exaggerate the benefits of state spending and understate their costs.[49]

Scholars who follow the public choice model attribute the existence of corruption primarily to 'a lack of competition in either or both economic and political arenas'.[50] Government officials usually enjoy high levels of discretion in regulating economic markets and this gives them the ability to extract bribes from the private sector. Greater government intervention results in the risk of corrupt behaviour increasing. To reduce corruption, attention must therefore be given to reducing levels of governmental intervention in the economy and the number of officials with discretion over economic policy.[51] Susan Rose-Ackerman, in a recent landmark study, argues strongly for competition among both politicians and bureaucrats to minimize corruption.[52] If politicians face the prospect of not being returned to office in democratic elections, or if civil servants are placed in a competitive situation in terms of services they offer, the incentives for malfeasance will be lower. Higher wages also play a critical role in this approach as they serve to provide the bureaucrat with job security which he or she will not ordinarily want threatened. It is also believed that democratic legislators will be more willing to pass anti-corruption legislation than authoritarian leaders, and that the 're-election' imperative actually lowers the imperative for bribes.[53] Increased levels of transparency in monitoring public conduct ensure that officials will minimize their corrupt practices.

In the African context, John Mbaku has argued for the application of the public choice model as a strategic alternative to previously failed attempts to tackle corruption. Following economist Douglas North, he maintains that a society's incentive systems are determined by its institutions, which in turn 'shape the behaviour of individuals who participate in political and economic markets, and determine the outcomes that are generated by markets and other forms of socio-political interaction'.[54] To change market outcomes, one must first change the relevant incentive systems. Thus, 'to increase productivity, innovation, and efficient allocation of resources in an economy', one must change from rent-seeking and related opportunistic behaviour to behaviour encouraging entrepreneurial activities that generate wealth.[55] If corruption as opportunistic behaviour continues to flourish, it implies that the existing rules of society are ineffective and in need of reform. Therefore efforts to control corruption must involve 'a negotiated change of the rules that results in the alteration of the existing incentive structure'.[56] Constitutionalism then becomes an almost divine imperative as the scramble begins to get a society to adopt a 'self-enforcing constitution' or 'social contract' that is mutually beneficial to all citizens.[57] Furthermore, if no respect is accorded to such values as personal choice, the right to private property and freedom of exchange, any reforms effected are unlikely to succeed in curbing corruption.

Case study: Zimbabwe – corruption notebook

A number of top-ranking Zimbabwean politicians, some of them government ministers, were named as having corruptly acquired vast tracts of lands, in some cases more than one farm each during the government's controversial and often violent land reform program over the past three years. The government of President Robert Mugabe conceded defeat in 2000 in a crucial national referendum on a proposed new constitution, and his party nearly lost a parliamentary election four months later to an opposition political party that was less than a year old. Realizing the popularity of the ruling ZANU-PF Party had declined, the government introduced the land redistribution program, seeking to immediately transfer vast tracts of rich commercial farms from ownership by a few thousand white farmers into the hands of the largely landless black peasant population.

By the time Mugabe, who has repeatedly been censured for condoning endemic corruption and protecting corrupt cronies within his government, ordered an audit of all the land acquired for rural resettlement, his controversial land-redistribution plan had clearly gone awry. Well-heeled ruling party politicians and business tycoons aligned to ZANU-PF had embarked on a frenzy of corrupt land acquisition, in some cases driving poor peasant farmers off the land on which they had recently been resettled. The Land Reform and Resettlement Program National Audit report named three cabinet ministers, four provincial governors, two leading businessmen and members of Mugabe's own family as having obtained farms through corrupt allocations. The audit was secretly coordinated in the office of Vice President Joseph Msika.

'We are not surprised by this report at all,' Wilfred Mhanda, chairman of the Zimbabwe Liberators' Platform, said soon after the shocking contents of the report were leaked to the press. 'It is what we've said all along, that the land seizures were benefiting those high up in ZANU-PF.' The Zimbabwe Liberators' Platform draws its membership from former liberation war fighters under Mugabe, who are now disillusioned by and disenchanted with the rampant corruption, mismanagement of the economy, and the violence and gross abuse of human rights that have become the hallmark of their former party, 20 years after attainment of independence.

(Extract from Geoffrey Nyarota, *Global Integrity Report 2004*, <http://www.globalintegrity.org/reports/2004/ 2004/countryf93e.html?cc=zw&act=notebook>.)

The experience of a number of developing countries would seem to confirm the view that the absence of competition and heavy state intervention in an economy tends to facilitate the spread of corruption.[58] Pranab Bardhan has reviewed the issue of incentive pay structure for civil servants, and finds it to be more complex than is suggested by public choice theorists. In the case of controlling corruption in a customs agency, for example, he argues that there is no point paying higher wages (to control corruption) if such a step adversely affects the price one ends up paying for an imported product.[59] Having a strong regulatory framework in place for the market economy to function at optimal level is also not the same as having guarantees that laws and property rights will be respected, as disrespect quickly leads to disloyalty and theft among public officials. Much of the public choice literature assumes that all states are predatory, but this does not help explain why corruption is more prevalent in some countries than in others with similar patterns of state intervention. The same countries might also differ with regard to levels of productivity and economic growth despite being equally corrupt.[60] State intervention to support certain types of industry and service, or to control imports and exports or fund large public works contracts, all provide opportunities for further corruption. But if the state intervenes to ensure fair competition internationally – as the USA does with its anti-trust legislation ostensibly to contain the power of monopolies for the welfare of its society against Europe, and its protectionist trade measures against Japan by the imposition of quotas and tariffs to safeguard businesses – or chooses to insist on a minimum wage, affirm the right of trade unions, or provide welfare services, such intervention might help to enhance 'the normative strengths of the "good society", and thus help to restrain or to offset corruption'.[61] Public choice principles for economic growth, as attractive as they appear, may therefore be contingent upon their application only in certain contexts.

Modifications to the functionalist model

The functionalist (or revisionist or structuralist) approach of establishing the possible benefits of corruption was initially common among political scientists. Up until the 1997 Asian financial crisis, some economists also flirted with this view, particularly in the context of South East Asia's rapid economic expansion in spite of, or because of, corruption. Indonesia might have been used as an example where institutional corruption and a low degree of uncertainty were more constructive for growth than less rampant corruption and a high degree of uncertainty. Vito Tanzi of the IMF provides a useful survey in this regard and mentions some of the main contributors to this position whose views we shall mention briefly.[62] On the question of time, it was argued by some that it held different values for different individuals, depending on one's income and how much one valued one's time. Thus, those who valued time the most would be willing to pay the highest bribes to jump the queues and have their decisions made quickly in the interests of efficiency. Corruption could serve as a 'useful political glue' by allowing politicians to secure funds that could in turn be used to keep a country stable for growth. Or, bribes could be used to supplement low wages and thus lower the government's tax burden, which was supposed to favour economic growth.[63] In the realm of procurement, it was considered possible that the most efficient firms would be those willing to pay the highest bribes, and so government projects would be tendered to them for efficiency's sake.

Tanzi, however, has cogently countered these arguments.[64] First, he indicates that rules are not created regardless of context and are not monolithic to a society. Rules that might ostensibly favour the practice of bribery are often intentionally devised to discourage such payments and more rules can easily be created so that power always resides with those who enforce them. Second, bribe-payers are not necessarily the most efficient but those who are most successful at rent-seeking. The higher the bribe, the higher the rate of return must be. The most productive individuals will be diverted into rent-seeking activities rather than being focused on socially productive activities and corruption will arise as a cost to society. Third, payment of speed money to save time can also have the effect of slowing down the whole process (through time spent on negotiating a bribe for instance), thus causing inefficiency. Political glue and wage supplements, while seemingly useful in the short term, can easily evaporate in the longer term, particularly in times of high inflation and political turmoil.

In an interesting study, Philippe Le Billon of the University of British Columbia in Canada has examined the role of corruption in armed conflicts.[65] He mentions that violent forms of competitive corruption between factions 'fuel war' by rewarding belligerents, while the 'buying-off' of the same belligerents can facilitate peaceful transition.[66] Le Billon shows that 'sticks' (such as economic sanctions) rather than 'carrots' have been frequently used in conflict resolution and believes the key challenge is 'to shift individual incentives and rewards away from the competition for immediate corrupt gains'.[67] His solution is to place public revenues under international supervision during peace operations. Corruption in situations of armed conflict does not necessarily lead to 'an historical path of developmental failure' but can be 'the most efficient means for individuals or groups to cope with a political economy of high uncertainty, scarcity and disorder through the proper cultivation of social relations'.[68] Fighting corruption is not advised as it 'may lead to anarchy rather than economic efficiency by destabilizing the existing hierarchy and order', while leaving corruption intact 'can sustain a degree of stability and even peaceful consensus when it is politically savvy and economically benign'.[69] Le Billon's argument is one that might have held sway for life in apartheid South Africa when petty corruption would have helped disenfranchised civil servants, usually at the bottom rung of civil service, to survive economic hardship when some of their bureaucratic practices seemed questionable.

Are we any closer to understanding corruption?

It is possible in the light of the preceding discussion on approaches to the study of corruption to conclude that the world has come of age in understanding corruption. One may also decipher an evolutionary thread that has prevented the global debate from degenerating into an amorphous heap of speculative innuendo. This thread began with a religiously orthodox and ideologically loaded conception of who was corrupt and where such culprits usually lived. But it soon progressed to one that recognized the universality of the practice, particularly as it originated in many cases from traditional cultural forms and norms of society. As the world began increasingly to modernize, some countries that were making the transition struggled and found alternative ways of coping with changes being imposed on them as their citizens scrambled through corrupt means to find their place in the sun. But, as people soon began to see, corruption had become a common way of cheating your boss, who knew little about you or your actual job, especially if you worked in a large organization. Previous attempts to control corruption were failing until experts started to realize that institutions and rules should be targeted for reform in a competitive environment. Some cases of corruption 'successes' might have resurfaced, but these were short-lived. The thread had in some way now come full circle, back to the notion that corruption is usually wrong – not inherently so, as some moralists believed, but because of the consequences it has for the sustainability of the market economy which is the heartbeat of the developing world. It is now very much a threat for all of humanity wherever it exists and the challenge of 'fighting' corruption in all its forms is increasingly part of most national strategies for good governance and political stability.

It needs to be mentioned that this chapter's survey of attempts to explain the nature of corruption and the forms that it takes should not be viewed as comprehensive by any means. Rather, it is intended to highlight approaches that have been shared by more than just one author from one particular setting and which have been routinely mentioned in the global debate on corruption. Most of these have contributed in no small way to helping us understand how corruption has been studied and observed throughout the world. The names of writers mentioned largely reflect the attention given to the subject by university scholars, but also show evidence, to a lesser degree, of contributions by public officials, development consultants and theologians. The extent to which their views might be useful in helping one devise and monitor a strategy to counter corruption is another, although related, matter to which we must return later. This is not an attempt to offer an historical overview of inaction on the part of churches towards corruption, as the notion of 'fighting corruption' in the world has only arisen as a governmental challenge for policy intervention since the 1970s; it is not mentioned anywhere before that time and thus most of the references in this book belong to the later modern period. The above survey or understanding provides an important precursor to our consideration of the extent to which the matter of costs and benefits in fighting corruption has been mostly neglected. While the reasons for such neglect will be discussed later, it should be noted here that the paucity of studies on the question of costs and benefits in any world context is quite a matter of concern when that question is (or should be) applied to matters of governance in the developing world.

Part 2

CONTROLLING CORRUPTION

3

Ways and means of fighting corruption

The task of fighting corruption in a developing country will in most cases require a particular strategy or approach (a way), matched by a commitment of resources (the means), to be successful. If corruption as a matter of scientific inquiry began to surface in the 1970s, so too did the debate about the most effective measures to contain its spread. This might have arisen partly as a result of the establishment of an independent state agency to fight corruption in Hong Kong during the 1970s, an initiative often upheld by scholars and practitioners alike as international best practice.[1] In addition, a range of ways to combat and prevent corruption emerged thereafter that were advocated for adoption in the developing world by foreign governments and their funding agencies for social, economic and humanitarian assistance, e.g. the United States Agency for International Development (USAID), the UK Department for International Development (DFID), etc. Most of these had evolved through the efforts of Transparency International (TI, see p. 10), and later the World Bank and the United Nations, in raising awareness about the need to fight corruption globally. It is helpful to briefly understand the main elements of these 'national integrity systems' (NISs), which we shall discuss later, as these had mostly been devised by the time newer democratic nations began to grapple with their own approaches to tackling corruption. The matter of locating the question of costs and benefits, within the broad sphere of public management, needs to be initially addressed here. If human, and more importantly financial, resources are required to ensure efficacy in the fight against corruption, one assumes that some form of calculation will be involved in determining their impact on the national resources of a country. It is of course possible that measures against corruption are enacted without due consideration to their budgetary implications, and that costs may be unwittingly incurred, or wittingly avoided in the process of devising new laws to fight corruption. Exactly where fighting corruption stands as a priority goal in the calculation of a country's total budget will be critical.

As may be clear to some, the benefits that arise from fighting corruption far outweigh the costs provided one accepts that a zero-tolerance approach is not achievable and that some corruption will have to be tolerated. In the case of Hong Kong, however, an enormous outlay of resources was rewarded with a drastic reduction in corruption levels, and the subsequent production of economic benefits. It seems logical, therefore, that the discussion on the ways to fight corruption be substantially informed by the available means at the disposal of the state, as the one is contingent upon the other. Even if one invests unlimited resources in fighting corruption, tangible benefits to society are not guaranteed unless one chooses the most appropriate strategy. Whether deciding on the way to fight corruption, or on the allocation of resources to do so, any decisions need to be implemented by public policy. Such decisions are never made in a vacuum and for this reason careful consideration will be given to some relevant international conventions (like the United Nations Convention against Corruption) and models available for the formulation of public policy. In this regard the focus of attention will be on Herbert Simon's rational decision-making model, and the critique of its limitations by an alternative model known as incrementalism. With this latter model we shall also observe its particular application in the process of budgeting and see why it continues to be a challenge for the governments of developing nations. To move to a more values-based approach to budgeting, where government spending is identified according to a set of negotiated priorities, is the critical test. The ways and means of fighting corruption have been tried and tested in many contexts, but it requires a creative tension and balancing act on the part of any government to find the middle ground between strategic imperatives and budgetary constraints. The international policy context has to a greater degree created a framework for developing nations to respond to the challenges of globalization, which among others, requires sovereign states to comply with particular conventions and protocols which in many cases are intended to combat and prevent corruption. Such instruments, particularly those dealing with corruption, will also be briefly mentioned as they provide a useful policy imperative for developing nations that rush to keep in synch with their peers by signing such promissory declarations. Finally, we consider in detail the case of Hong Kong, where corruption was successfully tackled using a three-pronged approach and which is, as mentioned above, often held up as an example of best practice.

Is a rational approach possible?

Choosing to fight corruption anywhere in the developing world would ordinarily involve a decision based on a public policy imperative. One does not choose to fight corruption in the absence of evidence of its existence, and in cases where it does rear its ugly head, the public demand for decisive action cannot be indefinitely ignored. But what is public policy and how is it best devised? From the 1960s, public policy as a specific area of analysis began to develop as a related field to and within public administration.[2] The definitions can be disparate, hence one approach is to distinguish between analysis *of* policy, which is academic and descriptive, looking at how policy is made, and analysis *for* policy, an applied and prescriptive activity that seeks to explain how a specific policy should be made.[3] What has become known as the 'rational' model of policy analysis was first advocated by renowned American scholar and Nobel Prize winner Herbert Simon in 1945 and relates directly to this discussion of costs and benefits. Simon developed a 'behaviour alternative model' which requires that when making a rational policy decision, an administrator (usually working in government) should first examine all policy options available, establish the consequences of each policy alternative, identify the benefits and costs of each course of action, and then choose an option that would provide the greatest net satisfaction of benefits over costs.[4] Such an approach would ensure that policy considerations are framed according to a maximizing norm of social gain, that is, 'governments should choose policies resulting in gains to society that exceed costs by the greatest amount, and governments should refrain from policies if costs are not exceeded by gains'.[5] Also, importantly, this rational model involves 'the calculation of all social, political, and economic values sacrificed or achieved by a public policy' and not just those that can be measured in monetary terms.[6] The diagram of how such a model is intended to work is shown in Figure 3.1.

In seeking 'optimal' courses of action to reconcile conflicting values and alternative points of view, Simon adopts a 'satisficing' position which requires that 'we look for *good enough* solutions

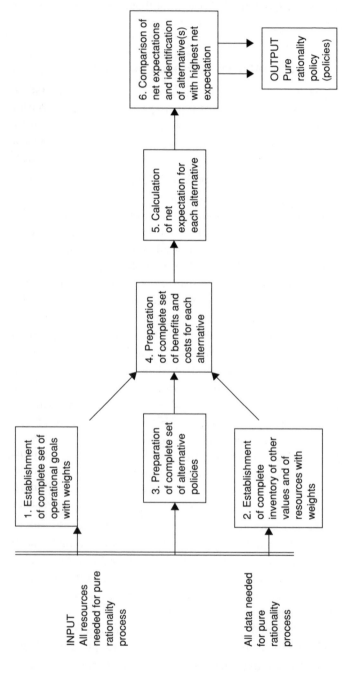

Figure 3.1 Rational model of policy analysis

Reproduced from Thomas R. Dye 1995, *Understanding Public Policy*, eighth edition, Englewood Cliffs, NJ: Prentice Hall, p. 29.

rather than insisting that only the best solutions will do'.[7] Members of an organization work for 'satisficing' (or satisfactory) solutions to problems faced in the workplace. It should be emphasized that Simon himself understood his behavioural model to be one which 'postulates that human rationality is very limited, very much bounded by the situation and by human computational powers'.[8] He complemented his model much later (after coming to terms with its limitations, as we shall see) with insights from psychology via 'intuitive theory', which recognizes the role of emotion in decision-making and underlines 'the skills humans can acquire by storing experience and by recognizing situations in which their experience is relevant and appropriate'.[9] Simon's rational model shows evidence therefore of development from a concern with pure rationality to the need for finding 'satisficing' solutions, to the 'melding of psychological theories of motivation and economic modeling techniques' in order to advance the study of decision-making.[10]

One is tempted to immediately seek the application of the rational model in formulating a policy decision to fight corruption. If corruption is usually harmful to society and creates social costs, the efforts to fight it or have it reduced will also involve costs. This leads Klitgaard to conclude that 'in most cases, the minimum cost solution will not have corruption equal to zero or anti-corruption efforts equal to the maximum amount'.[11] As far as calculating the optimal amount of corruption, Klitgaard further explains as follows: 'Imagine a function that relates the marginal social cost of a unit of corrupt activity to the total amount of that corrupt activity present in the society or organization. The very first unit of corruption may carry little social cost. But as corruption gets worse and worse – as the total amount of the corrupt activity grows larger – each additional unit may have ever greater social costs.'[12] He uses as an example a case where 'the costs might grow in such terms as breaking down norms of behaviour, creating greater inefficiencies, worsening the distribution of incomes and power, and so forth'.[13] The upward sloping line (see Figure 3.2) captures this result. On the other hand, one can imagine with Klitgaard the marginal social cost of reducing corruption as follows: 'If there were only a few instances of corrupt behaviour, they might be very costly to detect. On the other hand, if corruption were widespread, detection might be easier, and taking steps that reduced corruption by one unit might be relatively cheap. We might, then, hypothesize a declining marginal cost curve for reducing

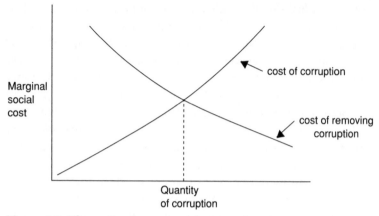

Figure 3.2 The optimal amount of corruption

Reproduced from Robert Klitgaard 1998, *Controlling Corruption*, Berkeley: University of California Press, p. 26.

corruption.'[14] This can be illustrated with a downward sloping curve (as shown in Figure 3.2).

To reduce corruption one would therefore be required to choose an approach and undertake a balancing exercise that would result in 'the greatest net satisfaction of benefits over costs' as described above. Such a task will usually prove quite difficult, if not impossible, to accomplish, for a number of reasons. First, to effect a cost calculation where the optimal level of corruption is not zero would require that 'society's value preferences' and their corresponding weights are known.[15] Second, all the policy options would have to be known in advance of a strategic approach being adopted. Third, the consequences of each policy option would have to be clearly identified beforehand, and lastly, the most 'efficient' policy option would have to be chosen. The need for comprehensive information, predictive capacity, administrative intelligence and the existence of a proper decision-making system to achieve a rational decision makes the balancing exercise mentioned above quite complex. Thomas Dye has observed that 'there are so many barriers to rational decision-making that it rarely takes place in government'.[16] Among these barriers, he mentions that social benefits cannot normally be agreed upon except those specific to individuals or groups, which of themselves can be conflicting. Benefits and costs defy weighting or comparison for the most part, and administrators are not motivated by social goals in making decisions but by personal interests of power, status, money and re-election.[17] To show that progress is being made, they will not find the 'one best way', but will settle for an alternative that will work.

This was something that Simon himself realized when it became obvious that his 'maximizing administrator' was utopian, that organizations tended to become sluggish and rigid while remaining in a state of equilibrium and that they changed only under strong pressures and then with little innovation.[18] Information gathering, which is vital for rational policymaking, is costly, not easily done and time consuming.[19] This factor is critical in the light that an organization's information flow does not generally relate to its information needs, that right information comes in unusable forms or too late to be useful, and that organizations tend to provide information which is not needed for policymaking.[20] Furthermore, modern organizations put much emphasis on division of labour and specialization of function, which gets in the way of a holistic approach to management of a single problem.[21] If different aspects of a problem are handled by different parts of an organization, co-ordination of their problem-solving efforts is usually less than perfect. Instead of taking a comprehensive perspective, problems will be viewed with narrower departmental 'spectacles'.[22] This failure stems from the inability to look beyond one's immediate horizon to a broader picture. For Simon therefore, the task of administrative science is to investigate the causes of 'bounded rationality', that is, the reasons why correct decisions are not taken.[23]

The classic administrator's dilemma is captured by Simon with his illustration of the fire chief who 'will attend primarily or perhaps exclusively to the problems of preventing and extinguishing fires, and will usually seek funds for improved equipment if such becomes available'.[24] But the 'rational' fire chief 'ought to consider whether his engines cause more harm through road accidents than they do good through getting to fires quickly; and he ought to ask himself whether the money he wants for new equipment would not be better spent upon hospitals or roads'.[25] Even in decisions about production and inventories, 'when practical decision-makers are observed in action, the forecasting-planning approach is sometimes conspicuous by its absence' as they appear to be '*reacting* to situations as they develop'.[26] One will hesitate to disagree with Simon here about his emphasis that administrators should look beyond their territorial domains, but he offers no criteria to the administrator to help quantify costs and benefits in maximizing community values. His 'bounded rationality' stance, if adopted, would seem to require that 'all decisions be made centrally which are interrelated in respect of either their goals or their resources'.[27] This would be possible, since the total value of public expenditure decisions can only be optimized (within his 'satisficing' framework) through integrated planning.

Thus, before a decision is made by a central bureaucracy, a search will ideally be undertaken to consider alternatives and ensure that such a decision accords with the organization's values. Yet Simon, the astute student of public administration, is keenly aware of the disadvantages of centralization as well.

Incrementalism

The limitations of the rational model of policymaking prompted political scientist Charles Lindblom to devise an alternative model of 'incrementalism' in 1959.[28] Lindblom argued for a more practical and comparative method of choosing between simplified alternatives to reflect how policy decisions are made in the real world.[29] In essence, according to Cameron, incrementalism 'holds that policies are made within a narrow spectrum of possible alternatives as administrators usually do not have the time, intelligence and money to investigate all policy alternatives and their consequences'.[30] Instead of adopting the optimal policy, they will stop at one that appears to work, which will effectively be a continuation of past government policy with incremental modifications. In a developing country lacking skilled personnel, accurate and reliable information, and sufficient financial resources, such a scenario can be quite severely debilitating.

Again, in Dye's description of incrementalism (which Simon would agree with), 'constraints of time, information, and cost prevent policymakers from identifying the full range of policy alternatives and their consequences' while the constraints of politics 'prevent the establishment of clear-cut societal goals and the accurate calculation of costs and benefits'.[31]

Incrementalism thus involves a conservative approach where 'policymakers generally accept the legitimacy of established programmes and tacitly agree to continue previous policies'.[32] It seeks to overcome the inefficiencies that result when the time and cost of developing policy might be excessive, as is often the case. Incrementalism seems to hold particular application, however, for budget making as well, as we shall now see.

Spending implications

Public institutions, like those engaged in fighting corruption, justify their existence, according to Koos Pauw and others, 'by the outputs that they produce to meet the benefits or outcomes that the people or their governments desire. One or more activity produces these outputs. The undertaking of all activities requires resources. Resources cost money.'[33] This gives rise to an expenditure budget ('a plan authorizing the expenditure of money to achieve public goals for a specific fiscal year'), which is 'a result of the need for resources that will be used in producing outputs to satisfy prioritized needs.'[34] Incrementalism, as discussed above, has traditionally supplied the framework for budgeting because 'decision-makers generally consider last year's expenditures as a base and limit active consideration of budget proposals to new items or requested increases over the base'.[35] However, Wildavsky cautions against aspects of incrementalism where alternative approaches to expenditure are only considered by those lower down in the hierarchy who will end up making the real decisions, based on outdated and uncertain information.[36] Not surprisingly then, with the introduction of the Public Finance Management Act in a newly created democracy like South Africa, the emphasis in the national budgeting process shifted to the question of value, such that strategic and operational plans are now required to inform the budget process.[37] The strategic plan indicates the work outputs that will lead to achieving a set of desired outcomes, while the operational plan provides the details about the resources to be used and the anticipated expenditure. Because budgets can be and are used to determine government priorities (and vice versa), they serve as the means 'to give financial muscle to those priorities'.[38]

The problem with budgeting, according to Peter Self, 'is to know how the benefits of public expenditure are to be defined, determined and quantified'.[39] If one followed the rational model strictly and adhered to a narrow economist's version of cost-benefit analysis, a budget would be produced by a central agency which would be qualified to determine all relevant costs and benefits in monetary terms. All economic, social and political values would have to be calculated, and in theory it would not be possible to increase benefits unless they were weighted against their potential costs. But the problem of attributing monetary value to saving the life of someone on a dialysis machine over against a tax increase, for example, can be highly subjective as 'there is no yardstick which can comprehend all the values that are relevant to policy decisions'.[40] Two other complications arise, according to Self. Politicians and other actors in the budgetary process 'are usually reluctant to make their values explicit, and prefer perhaps necessarily to work with conflicting or ambivalent goals. Additionally, the framework for ordering the values is itself a subject of dispute or uncertainty'.[41]

For the above reasons then, it seems obvious that government spending is more about 'limits, choices and trade-offs' as the process of 'weighing up the relative importance of one programme against another' in terms of the public agenda is played out.[42] The competing interests that constitute the public agenda, however, are so numerous and entail so wide a range of governmental action that 'comprehensive policy analysis becomes truly impossible', yet a budget must be produced.[43] Unfortunately though, as Gildenhuys has noted, the 'comparison between cost and programme value, vital to intelligent resource allocation, is not a regular component of budget resource processes.'[44] It seems plausible to believe that 'the calculation of the exact amounts to be allocated when the money is divided between programmes in the light of the various general goals is very complicated indeed'.[45]

If the demand for prioritization requires that trade-offs be made, between and within government departments, 'reprioritization' is necessary in order to change spending patterns so that they reflect those of the new government over against the imbalances usually inherited from the past.[46] In the attempt to do more with less, it is important that there is 'accessible information about what trade-offs are being made, what everybody stands to gain or lose, what the future benefits would be and to whom they would accrue'.[47] It is equally important that the budget be comprehensive enough; if extra-budgetary funds are needed or certain expense items excluded (as is the case when resources to fight corruption are considered), the task of making decisions about directing expenditure towards achieving new strategic results becomes more difficult. The problem of unfunded mandates (i.e. directives from national government to provincial and local government given without supporting funds) also arises here. One way of dealing with this situation is 'to enact legislation which compels costing ("fiscal noting") to be made before mandates are implemented', or for the lower-level tiers of government to claim reimbursement for costs incurred in implementing unfunded mandates.[48] The net benefit of each institutional activity can be used to determine priorities, with the activity showing the highest net benefit receiving the highest priority and so forth.[49] The budget of the education department in a developing country, for example, might show a steady increase year on year as it remains committed to producing a skilled workforce to meet its growing needs. Groups representing different stakeholders will still need to be consulted 'throughout the process of determining costs and benefits and for negotiations on the institution's final choice of priorities'.[50] This is critical, especially as an objective view of priorities among the various stakeholders with 'interests' will not be possible. This scenario, of the complexity of a democratic budgeting process, presents one of the most enduring challenges for developing nations if they are to adequately fund the fight against corruption.

Public priorities for government spending are usually not static and will be reprioritized if budgeting becomes a (democratic) 'process', where consensus is sought over diverse interests which are then factored into a quantification of costs and benefits such as that discussed above. The notion of a public agenda becomes pertinent if one is to consider what the most pressing problems that government should address are, and whether such problems as articulated by the citizens generally have been prioritized previously. Public opinion obviously counts for a lot in a democracy: when a government finds itself on a collision course with such opinion, the likelihood of it being returned to office can be severely tested. The 'bad news' about public spending, however, remains, as Pauw and others have noted, in that 'even if we know the things we are of necessity to finance, and even if we know which programmes are the most important for us, we cannot be sure of how to translate that into amounts of money'.[51] If the programme of fighting corruption is identified as a key government activity, in whatever order of priority, and is listed in strategic or operational plans, it will therefore require such 'amounts of money' if it is to be implemented despite the web of budgetary complexity surrounding it.

National integrity systems

If one assumes that funding is available in whatever amounts to fight corruption, the next question to be asked is how such resources can be effectively used to produce maximum benefits. The discussion now shifts therefore to the ways of fighting corruption. When TI was formed in 1993, its intention was based on a general principle that it would not deal with single and specific cases of corruption, but attempt 'to develop and strengthen the structural framework' in countries across the world.[52] From debate and discussions within the TI movement, there emerged during its early years the concept of a 'national integrity system' (NIS) to improve standards of governance.[53] This was in essence a holistic system designed to promote transparency and 'horizontal accountability' in all spheres of the public sector, but requiring the active participation of civil society (via such groups as charities, faith-based formations, community groups and trade unions) and with a decisive role to be played by the private sector. It was also meant to act 'as a practical way to avert the damage which corruption causes to the public interest and as a way of fostering an environment in which the quality of decision-making is heightened'.[54] The NIS approach was framed within the mainstream development agenda of the time, which prioritized the interests of the poor and marginalized in the context of an enabling state and which saw corruption as an obstacle to that goal. This made its usage among anti-corruption activists, governments, international institutions and aid donors quite common.[55] But it also required adaptation according to a country's socio-economic context and institutional arrangements, as the process of reform was itself often subject to manipulation for corrupt purposes. It was therefore necessary to allow for considerable flexibility in seeking to implement the NIS within the unfolding development shifts of a given country, so that it did not indirectly create more opportunities for new corrupt actors to stake their claim in the changing system.

The NIS assumes that modern government operations are required to be transparent and accountable, but in many countries making the transition to democracy, as well as those still developing, there existed a prevalence of autocratic rule. Elites with monopoly power would discharge orders and rules for implementation from a central point to those down the line. Over against such a system another was possible where power would be dispersed, no single person enjoying a monopoly position, and lines of 'horizontal account-ability' would be clearly drawn, a culture of transparency being its defining character. Such a 'virtuous circle' is thus the ideal, where 'each actor is both a watcher and is watched, is both a monitor and is monitored'.[56] From a system in which the only responsibility (under tyrannical rule) is vertical, one would shift to another where watchdog bodies and agencies of restraint exercise a careful check on the president and the executive, parliament, the courts, banks, the media, the public service and other institutions of government, with an appropriate role identified for civil society and the inter-national community. Each one of these entities, including the watch-dog agencies, constitutes a 'pillar' holding up the 'roof' of national integrity (see illustration of such a system in Figure 3.3). The period of transition from one system to the next can be quite slow and fraught with many obstacles, but the aim throughout must be to make corruption a 'high risk' and 'low return' activity that can be pre-vented, instead of relying on law enforcement after the fact.[57] Total dependence on a single pillar of integrity must be avoided, while gaps and weaknesses in the system must continuously be addressed to prevent a systems collapse. Corresponding rules and practices such as fair elections, conflict of interest rules, public service ethics, access to information, whistle-blowing legislation, etc., to sustain the pillars both individually and collectively, must be built into the system. The establishment and maintenance of any or all of the pillars will involve direct costs, a matter that is not addressed in any detail in the *TI Source Book*, except in the context of multilateral donor assist-ance, widespread by the late 1990s.

The impact of the NIS approach to fighting corruption had become widespread by 1995. By 1998 USAID had developed a framework to assist its missions around the world to help countries develop a strategy that would 'combine societal reforms to institu-tionalize political will with targeted institutional reforms'.[58] To ad-dress the unique forms of corruption in the former Soviet Union and Eastern Europe, the World Bank developed a multi-pronged strategy comprising five 'building blocks', namely, institutional restraints, political accountability, a competitive private sector, public sector management and civil society participation.[59] For the strategy to be effective, 'some guidelines for the selection and sequencing of reform priorities tailored to the particular contours of the corruption problem in each country' had to be developed, feasible entry points

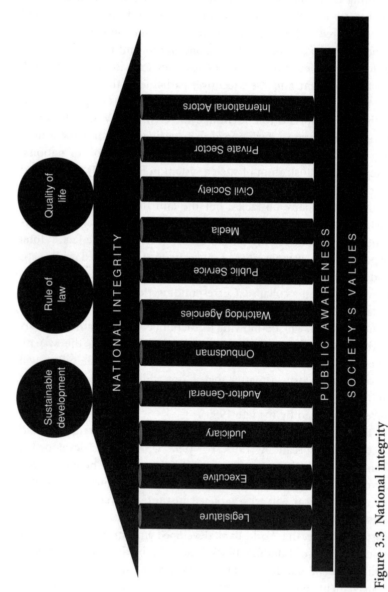

Figure 3.3 National integrity

Reproduced from Jeremy Pope (ed.) 2000, *Confronting Corruption: The Elements of a National Integrity System*, Berlin: Transparency International, p. 35.

identified, and coalitions of anti-corruption efforts assembled. In 2001 the Vienna-based United Nations Centre for Crime Prevention launched a Global Programme against Corruption with pilot projects in selected countries. A modular approach was adopted, a broad set of 'tools' being used to cover prevention, enforcement, institution building, awareness raising, anti-corruption legislation and monitoring.[60] The tools themselves were flexible enough to 'be utilized at different stages and levels, and in a variety of combinations according to the needs and context of each country or sub-region'.[61]

The experiences of many developing countries, and of these making a transition to democratic government and a free-market economy, where the NIS and such related approaches have been mostly implemented, however, suggest some serious shortcomings. While the NIS provides for a role to be played by international actors, these countries are often 'simply unable to deal with the problem of corruption without pressure and help' from this quarter; there is in fact 'a general absence of co-ordinated and sustained support by multilateral and bilateral donors for anti-corruption initiatives'.[62] While the NIS puts a high premium on home-grown initiatives, international pressure is a critical driver of anti-corruption programmes and plays an important role in providing civil society organizations with the means to fund their projects.[63] The dichotomy extends to these programmes themselves as well, which often use 'technocratic, generic, and broad language which means little to people in the field and to the general public' who are supposed to own the programmes.[64] Such language might act as cover, 'giving the donors the right to engage in political activity under the guise of technocratic intervention'.[65] Some of the 'best practices' advanced have no history of practical success, and can sometimes be so complicated that it is difficult to prove their usefulness or uselessness. In search of new anti-corruption 'markets' donors have steered the agenda to be so broad that now 'it encompasses all parts of social, political and economic life'.[66] An inordinate and unnecessary amount of resources have been directed towards the measurement or quantification of corruption, which can be a most dubious exercise, rather than towards efforts to strengthen the pillars of integrity. Future implementation of the NIS in the developing world will continue to require more adequate resources to sustain anti-corruption initiatives, more effective co-ordination among donors, greater international pressure where necessary, and a stronger civil society sector that will hold governments accountable.

Yet, because its multifaceted approach involves different pillars and a host of stakeholders, all not necessarily working towards the same goal at the same time, its use may be challenged by a narrower law enforcement option where a single institution takes centre stage for the sake of cost-effectiveness.

International action against corruption

Any country contemplating action against corruption for the first time can now, unlike two decades ago, subscribe to challenges posed by new international instruments that require consenting nations to agree to undertake a series of reforms to contain the spread of corruption. One of the first was a United Nations Code of Conduct for International Public Officials, adopted in 1997 to provide member states with 'a tool to guide their efforts against corruption through a set of basic recommendations that national public officials should follow in the performance of their duties'.[67] This was followed by the Declaration against Corruption and Bribery in International Commercial Transactions and, later, the adoption in 2000 of the United Nations Convention against Transnational Organized Crime, which included several provisions related to corruption. These initiatives paved the way for further discussions among member states on the need for an effective international legal instrument against all aspects of corruption. After two years of negotiations, the United Nations Convention against Corruption was adopted in Mexico in December 2003, thus creating 'the first global instrument embracing a comprehensive range of anti-corruption measures to be taken at the national level'.[68] A wide range of measures to prevent and combat corruption are proposed, which leads TI to conclude that 'many countries will require considerable help to take the necessary steps to implement it'.[69] Whether such help or 'technical assistance' is forthcoming remains to be seen, but apart from that, the UN Convention has certainly set a global standard for developing countries to emulate if they are to compete with their developed counterparts, whose access to financial resources to fight corruption is, of course, much less constrained.

The Organization for Economic Co-operation and Development (OECD) Convention on Combating Bribery of Foreign Public Officials in International Business Transactions was adopted in May 1997 by 29 member countries, and came into force from February 1999. Members would ordinarily be required to enact laws making foreign bribery a crime. By 2003, TI found that even 'though most laws have been in place for several years, most countries have taken little or no enforcement action' and warned that 'there is serious danger that the Convention will fail to become an effective weapon against international corruption'.[70] From information gathered from country reports and OECD experts, TI identified the following as one of the most common causes for the lack of enforcement of the OECD Convention:

> Investigating and prosecuting foreign bribery cases requires extensive work by experienced professionals. Law enforcement officers in many Convention countries are not adequately staffed or trained to undertake foreign bribery cases. Because most prosecutors are already swamped by large case loads, they are reluctant to take on new cases that require large resources and will take years to complete.[71]

The efficacy potential of the OECD instrument against corruption was thus still being questioned five years after it came into force because insufficient resources were being committed for its implementation.

In the case of the Southern African Development Community (SADC) Protocol against Corruption, the overall situation is much worse. This protocol was meant to be a significant instrument in the multilateral approach to fighting corruption. The key challenge of reforming anti-corruption legislation across the SADC region to bring it in line with the protocol, however, has floundered. The protocol was signed in August 2001, but has yet to be ratified by the requisite number of member countries (two-thirds) to come into force. Roger Batty, who worked for anti-corruption agencies in Hong Kong, Botswana and South Africa, believed the problem to be linked to a 'wide disparity throughout the region as to the volume of resources devoted to national anti-corruption campaigns'.[72] Also, he notes that 'in some nations there is no budget for such programmes and until this is addressed, little progress will be made'.[73] His solution is targeted at donor aid, which he says should be redirected towards supporting regional initiatives that encourage further self-development, cost-effective solutions and lasting results such as the facilitation of skills training.[74] Based largely on the SADC Protocol, the more recent African Union (AU) Convention on Preventing and Combating Corruption and Related Offences was adopted by African heads of state in July 2003. No fewer than 15 states must ratify the process before the AU Convention can come into force. While Article 19 of the Convention provides for consenting countries to work 'closely with international, regional and sub-regional financial organizations to eradicate corruption in development aid and co-operation pro-grammes', no further mention is made in the Convention of the need for resources to enable the fight against corruption to be effective.[75] This is ordinarily a matter for the consideration of member states individually, but if no budgets exist for such purposes, as is often the case (which is what Batty would have us believe), there is little hope of the AU Convention being effectively implemented and corruption reduced as a result.

The advent of a new world onslaught against corruption in the 1990s was accompanied by the creation of internationally accepted legal standards of conduct that would henceforth identify those countries that shared the political will to fight corruption. Yet as we have seen, signing or even ratifying a legal instrument does not in many countries translate into an allocation of resources to offset the costs that arise from implementing it. It would of course have been far more helpful, had it been possible, to use the method of cost-benefit analysis, for example, before consent were given by any country to the adoption of protocols like those mentioned above. One does not doubt that such 'compliance costs' will differ greatly from country to country, thus making the task of calculating costs against benefits all the more difficult. But a warning of possible abuse of the method and the process is in order here, as Wildavsky notes: 'To expect, however, that the method itself (which indulges some and deprives others) would not be subject to manipulation in the political pro-cess is to say that we shall be governed by formula and not by men. Because the cost-benefit formula does not always jibe with political realities – that is, it omits political costs and benefits – we can expect it to be twisted out of shape from time to time.'[76] Wildavsky's comments would be equally relevant if we were to hypothesize that the matter of costs has certain critical political connotations, or ramifications, depending on policy imperatives and political actors.

Hong Kong: an example of best practice

Let us now turn to a case that involved heavy monetary investment in the fighting of corruption, with beneficial results. When the Inde-pendent Commission Against Corruption (ICAC) was formed in Hong Kong in 1974, corruption had become deeply rooted in what was then a British colony. After World War II, the influx of immigrants from China gave rise to an acute shortage of services.[77] This created a situation where deprived citizens recognized that using personal ties or gifts to obtain public services improperly was officially wrong but socially acceptable. The numerous regulations and restrictions placed upon them by an 'alien government' were resented as the British comprised only one per cent of the population.[78] An Anti-Corruption Branch (ACB) was formed in 1952 within the Criminal Investigation Department, but proved highly ineffective, as it was too closely allied to the police force and members could end up investigating allegations against colleagues.[79]

The 1960s ushered in a tumultuous time of change for Hong Kong that saw the rise of social unrest and economic instability. The initial spark seems to have been caused by a fare increase for a ferry ride between Hong Kong Island and nearby Kowloon, which provoked public demonstrations that later turned into riots.[80] During the resultant hearings by government, allegations of police corruption often surfaced.[81] The cultural revolution had also broken out in China in 1966 and spread to Hong Kong. Workers and students took to the streets often in confrontation with the police, who risked their lives to maintain law and order. The economy was shaken as some banks closed down, leaving thousands deprived of their life savings. China was rising as a global power and many immigrant Chinese began to assert their origins, embracing the motherland with its communist doctrine of self-reliance, political impartiality and economic independence.[82] Corruption in these years proved a useful issue with which activists could attack the authorities.

The colonial government, it seems, 'was compelled to act promptly, to make changes, to restore its dwindling reputation, and to demonstrate to its critics the supremacy of colonialism over socialism'.[83] Moves were afoot to recognize Chinese as the second official language of the 'territory', rather than the colony, and government officials now sought to learn new ways of combating corruption from neighbouring states like Singapore. A new powerful ordinance was introduced in 1971 with the ACB becoming a semi-independent Anti-Corruption Office (ACO) reporting to the Assistant Commissioner of Police.[84] Corruption seemed to be under control for a while, until the sudden disappearance of police Chief Superintendent Peter Godber, who was being investigated by the ACO. He fled to England, leaving the authorities powerless under existing procedures, much to the outrage of the public. A commission of inquiry to be headed by Sir Alistair Blair-Kerr was subsequently appointed to look into the matter and suggest changes to the current anti-corruption measures.[85]

The decision to create ICAC was taken by the Hong Kong governor, Sir Murray MacLehose, soon after receiving the famous 'Blair-Kerr Report' in 1973. Lest people believe that his whole government was corrupt, he told the Legislative Council that 'the situation calls for an organization, led by men of high rank and status, which can devote its whole time to the eradication of this evil' of corruption. Public confidence in 'a unit that was entirely independent, and separate from any department of the government, including the police' was a prerequisite.[86] The police of course believed that it was their specialized task to investigate all acts of corruption and cautioned that such a step would have a 'disastrous effect' on their morale, but the decision was well received by the citizenry generally.[87] ICAC was to be established by statute, not simply by administrative act, and headed by a commissioner who would not be 'subject to the direction or control of any person other than the Governor'.[88] The expenses of the commission were to be provided for in the budget by a single expenditure vote. The three-pronged strategy against corruption was clearly outlined in the ICAC Ordinance, which required investigation, prevention and public education. The legal framework was also amended to allow, among other things, the confiscation of 'unexplained wealth', with the accused being presumed guilty until proven innocent, and the commissioner being allowed to seize assets suspected of being proceeds from corrupt practices. The question of an amnesty for past corrupt activity was not considered at this time, and this led to much disquiet until a partial amnesty was proclaimed for offences committed before 1997.[89] To ensure that the ICAC would not abuse its sweeping powers, 'an elaborate system of checks and balances was created to maintain oversight'.[90]

Bertrand de Speville, a former ICAC commissioner, credits the unparalleled success of the organization to the political will to fight corruption, a strong legal framework, effective strategy, active community involvement, government's willingness to persevere in fighting corruption and, of course, what he terms 'adequate and sustained funding'.[91] In this latter instance, ICAC's 'exceptional resources' outweighed anything of comparison elsewhere in the world. In 1974 it began with a budget of £1 million, which increased to £7 million by 1984, and by 1997 equated to about £38 million, while it employed 1,225 officials.[92] From surveys conducted to measure public perceptions, one may conclude, as LaMagna does, that 'the ICAC has achieved a high degree of success in rooting out corruption and in changing the culture of corruption' to one of 'lawfulness and a relatively clean society'.[93] Outputs in terms of investigations, arrests, prosecutions, publications and public awareness were undoubtedly high but, as Huberts observes, 'it is less clear what effect this output had on the actual level of corruption'.[94] More importantly, however, corruption was no longer accepted as a way of life or doing business in Hong Kong. In fact, the remarkable progress made in establishing Hong Kong as a leading financial and commercial centre in Asia is partly attributed to its success in fighting corruption.[95] Singapore remains the only other Asian country to score higher on TI's Corruption Perceptions Index (see Appendix), which is testimony to Hong Kong's strength as an environment in which to do 'clean business'. According to LaMagna, a law enforcement agent who worked for many years in Asia, 'The key to Hong Kong's success was the three-pronged approach, and the recognition that one element could not work without the others.'[96] For Commissioner Nin, the aspects of checks and balances, committed staff, and the independence of the ICAC were equally critical in his explanation of the organization's success.[97] It is not without reason therefore that this Hong Kong model of success in fighting corruption has been tried and tested in other parts of the world, as it is commonly regarded as international best practice.

Case study: Police corruption in Australia

Widespread corruption in Australia's police continues to arouse public concern in spite of major inquiries and reforms in the several states across the country. Following up on a campaign promise made by the Labour Party during the 2001 elections, a Royal Commission was established in Western Australia in December 2001 to look into allegations of police corruption. The 18-month inquiry opened in March 2002 with an offer of amnesty for any serving and former police officers who made a written tell-all confession about their knowledge of corrupt and criminal police activity before 31 May 2002 and were prepared to give evidence. In return they would be indemnified from prosecution, given anonymity and permission to resign and to keep accrued staff benefits and any ill-gotten gains. The Kennedy Inquiry, named after the former Supreme Court judge who was appointed to lead the commission, has been granted wide-ranging powers to investigate cases of corruption or criminal activity by any Western Australian police officer as far back as 1985.

The allegations of widespread corruption in Western Australia are not unique. Indeed, the Royal Commission in Western Australia is the third to look into police corruption in Australia in recent years. It follows the Fitzgerald Royal Commission in Queensland in the 1980s and the Wood Royal Commission in New South Wales in the 1990s. Both uncovered significant evidence of entrenched police corruption; one case led to the imprisonment and the other to the resignation of the police commissioner. More recently, in New South Wales, hearings held by the independent Police Integrity Commission, first set up in 1996, show that corruption in the police is still a serious problem. In April 2002, Police Commissioner Peter Ryan resigned abruptly amid charges that he had failed in his reform efforts. Police corruption is set to be an issue in the state elections of 2003.

In the state of Victoria, there are growing calls for a similar high-level investigation. Following an internal police investigation and concern about widespread corruption in the state's drug squad, the newly appointed chief commissioner, Christine Nixon, announced in December 2001 her intention to disband the squad. Those plans stalled, however, after protests from the police union. All these events have led to debate about why police corruption continues in an advanced industrialized country that has political will, public support and resources to curb it. Experts say that one of the reasons why police corruption is so widespread is an inherent 'police culture' that encourages unsavoury behaviour.

(Extract from Peter Rooke, 'Police Corruption Thriving in Australia', *Global Corruption Report 2003*, London: Profile Books on behalf of Transparency International, Berlin, 2003, p. 117.)

Making political choices

If public policy analysis is about 'who gets what' and 'why' and 'what difference it makes', as Thomas Dye suggests,[98] the foregoing discussion has in some way opened up space for one to ask why governments choose a particular strategy to confront corruption and what consequences such a policy stance will likely have. Not every single initiative by every state department or agency can be considered in isolation as having a direct or indirect impact on reducing corruption. Instead, a broader framework is to be preferred, one involving multiple interactions among groups and individuals (including churches) that eventually produces a sequence of decisions (or resolutions) requiring action and implementation. The consequences of such action (or inaction, as policy can be about what is not being done) are quite significant if one is to judge whether a policy option is reaching its intended target. We have seen that the rational model of making policy decisions has proven to be quite useful in raising the critical questions about the logic that should inform political choices. The insights of incrementalism were also found to be useful when the matter of budgetary scope and limits was considered. It was necessary also to examine some of the conventional wisdom about how integrity systems and international instruments can be built and applied in order to contain corruption. In a context where budgets are anything but an afterthought, though, the ways chosen to fight it were shown to be highly effective, provided that political will and community support were secured. The current approach and policy framework in a developing country, as far as fighting corruption is concerned, therefore warrants critical scrutiny if one is to compare and contrast situations where 'who gets what' and 'why' and 'what difference it makes' is contingent upon policy choice. Only after the debate about the measurement of competing options against local innovations has been qualitatively explored may one be permitted to speculate (or prescribe).

Corruption in the developing world has now become much more of a problem requiring government intervention than was the case 20 years ago. However, the nature of the problem is not one where a clear pronouncement can be made on the extent of corruption in any country. While the political will to fight corruption is not absent, as most political leaders would have us know, reticence on the part of any national government to commit funds from its treasury towards its control will prove detrimental to the prospect of reducing corruption in the long term. National strategies will be severely compromised by this failure to calculate monetary costs and make budgetary allocations for the fight against corruption. Unless the effort of confronting corruption is elevated as a line item (a single item shown on a separate line) or cost centre (a segregated part where someone can be held accountable for expenses without having to show a monetary profit) within a nation's budgetary cycle and is considered as a fiscal end in itself, the possibility that fighting corruption may produce a positive impact for society will recede. Governments must show they are serious, not just by signing anti-corruption conventions, but by investing resources towards its control.

4

Costs and benefits of
fighting corruption

Corruption around the world has become an increasing problem, requiring more intervention on the part of governments than was the case before the 1990s. Yet as our intention has not been to determine levels of corruption, no pronouncement has thus far been attempted on the actual extent of corruption, or why one country might be more corrupt than another. Instead, it is assumed that while the political will to fight corruption is not absent in most democratic societies, there remains a distinct reticence on the part of national governments to commit resources towards its control.[1] The national strategy to combat corruption, where it may exist, is as a result severely compromised by the failure to calculate monetary costs and make budgetary allocations for the fight against corruption. Unless this effort of fighting corruption is elevated as a line item within the national budgetary cycle and is considered as a fiscal end in itself, the possibility that fighting corruption may produce a positive impact for society will recede.

If and when a policy decision is taken to bring corruption under control in any given context, and fund the fight against it, the question will arise as to how and to which functions of government such funding will be apportioned. In a situation of diminishing resources and increasing budgetary constraints, the challenge to find an acceptable balance in adequately responding to the needs of the country becomes quite acute. Continued reliance on donor support to drive the strategy against corruption is unsustainable if costs escalate and a greater impact is sought. It behoves any government therefore to be more prudent in how it uses its existing resources. Here, we look at some scenarios that may arise when a national government exercises certain options in fighting corruption:

- The first is one where increased public spending will likely produce an increase in benefits (such as less corruption) but only if additional revenue can be procured (which at present seems unlikely for less developed countries).

- The second, which is offered more as a caution, is one where increased but arbitrary spending can actually cause a reduction in benefits (such as an over-emphasis on bureaucracy) and contribute to a negative overall impact.
- The third and final option, of decreased spending and increased benefits (such as less corruption), is obviously the least costly to implement but is more difficult to effect against administrative and political interference.

Of course, the role of civil society formations and faith communities can be crucial in pressuring governments to act in any one of the above ways.

To fully appreciate the tension posed by this juxtaposition of costs and benefits, it might help if we begin with an example of a story that is not uncommon in South Africa. On 19 August 2004, the *Pretoria News*[2] appeared with the front page headline, 'Massive probe of fake licences'. The article concerned a nationwide investigation that was to be launched into irregularities surrounding the issuing of thousands of drivers' licences. In the Greater Pretoria area alone, it was claimed that up to 20,000 drivers had been issued with fraudulent licences. Seventy investigators from the Special Investigating Unit (set up by government to deal with corruption-related cases) were to be assigned to the case, which was expected to last at least three years and cost the taxpayer £4 million. Using such resources, both human and financial, to investigate just one case may be thought extravagant if one considers that the annual budgets of individual anti-corruption agencies in other state departments are often smaller. If one went further and tabulated the costs of similar probes into corruption in customs, the Road Accident Fund, Correctional Services, the police service, procurement procedures in housing departments, money laundering, immigration control, the issuing of identity documents, birth certificates, passports and fishing licences, which have all been targets for corrupt practices, the total would probably run into many millions of pounds and require the services of hundreds of trained personnel. Clearly, all acts of corruption cannot be investigated with the same amount of resources set aside for the single national probe into fake licences. Corruption, it seems, does matter, but so does the lack of water and electricity in rural South Africa, anti-retroviral treatment for HIV/AIDS, classrooms for schools, clinics, sports facilities for the citizenry, parks and gardens in public places, better roads, formal housing for all, and so forth. The fight against corruption anywhere in Africa, and elsewhere in the world, has to compete with a long list of equally legitimate priorities within the budgetary constraints that determine the allocation of national resources.

Pay more, gain more

As mentioned earlier, it is very difficult to calculate the costs of fighting corruption. If it were possible, ideally each corruption case requiring investigation would be subject to a cost-benefit analysis and a budget. In reality, one assumes that investigations are being taken up despite the high costs. However, the political rhetoric about corruption has not been reinforced by a commitment of resources to make the fight against it effective.

Large-scale investigations

An increase in corruption, especially with regard to fake drivers' licences, necessitated a focused national anti-corruption initiative with very high cost implications for the state's treasury, as we saw. The obvious expected benefit from an exercise like this (if it actually took place) would be that only properly authorized drivers' licences issued in South Africa would be valid. Fake licences would be confiscated and those holding them, together with those involved in issuing them, would be prosecuted. South African roads would be safer for public use, as only legitimately qualified drivers would be allowed to use them, thus bringing down the already very high accident rate. Of course, the assumption being made here is that drivers with fake licences are more prone to causing accidents than those with legitimate licences. It is also assumed (incorrectly) that those who drive without any kind of licence (such as teenagers under the age limit) are less of a threat when they use the roads, often at high speed. Such a conclusion seems logical when such drivers are not targeted for investigation. Legitimately licensed drivers, it should be noted, can be a serious obstacle to public safety if they drive in vehicles that are not in roadworthy condition, which, again, is a common sight on South African roads. The point being made here is that the public benefit that is supposed to accrue from the massive investigation mentioned above is quite difficult to quantify, let alone justify, against other budgetary priorities that the country faces. Yet if the task of fighting corruption were viewed as a fiscal end in itself like, for example, spending on national defence or education, the question would hardly arise.

If government, on the other hand, decided to ignore the prevalence of corruption in the issuing of drivers' licences in order to save on resources, the situation that would arise would be equally untenable. Most citizens would soon become aware of the corruption and would be encouraged to bypass the law in obtaining their licences without following the rigorous procedures involved or paying the stipulated fees. After all, why should one pay more and subject oneself to a test when it can be bypassed and the fee negotiated? Before long, those who continuously profited from this form of corruption would want to increase their illicit income and would seek new ways of introducing corruption into other areas of service delivery, for example, in the issuing of fishing quota licences, work permits and identity documents. An antinomian culture would take root in society, inviting even organized crime to proliferate, and causing the rule of law to be severely compromised. Foreign direct investment would suffer as investors lost confidence in the ability of the government to make the country safe and the rules for business transactions certain. With decreased investment, levels of mass unemployment would rise, putting government under added pressure, and a general apathy towards law enforcement would become the order of the day. Such a scenario reflects to a considerable extent the reality in some countries of the developing world. South Africa, not wishing to suffer the same fate, therefore adopts a more proactive approach to fighting corruption by effecting counter-measures such as the one we are discussing here. While the benefits to society from the above 'clampdown' might not be immediately clear, the long-term benefits are far more convincing. Ignoring corruption, at zero cost, is thus not an option worth exploring, especially if one accepts that corruption is wrong of itself and must be combated.

Calculating the cost

The conventional wisdom about fighting corruption, as articulated by a noted scholar such as Robert Klitgaard,[3] requires that some kind of action (like that taken against the fake drivers' licence scam) must be taken. Klitgaard goes further and calls on countries to make a cost calculation such that the costs of fighting corruption do not outweigh the benefits derived from it. This is not something we would venture to question at first sight. Yet, because of the extreme complexity of such a task, Klitgaard himself is unable to offer an example of how a country can possibly make such a calculation at any given time. The insights of other scholars and specialists in the field of anti-corruption have failed to produce any new evidence to help make such a calculation.[4] It seems that one should instead be encouraged to accept that though attempting to calculate the costs of fighting corruption is a useful point of departure for preventing costs from exceeding benefits, the nature of corruption and the attempts to fight it defy the use of cost-benefit analysis for this purpose. The usually harmful effects of corruption are not disputed, nor is the need for action to be taken against it. Whenever and whatever action is contemplated, however, costs will arise that require a 'balancing act' on the part of government. The South African finance minister was reported in the *Pretoria News* as having said exactly this: 'The challenge of budgeting is not about all on social grants or all on road building, it is not about just spending on education versus spending all our money on fixing the ports. It is about managing this delicate balance.'[5] Government spending on fighting corruption in South Africa specifically has historically been minimal in comparison to other budgetary items. As a result the efficacy of its anti-corruption strategy has been compromised, but a case has not been made for government to increase such spending.

The introduction of a national integrity system[6] into a country suffering the effects of increased corruption offers the possibility of some management and control being exercised, to the extent that benefits will arise as the 'pillars of integrity' are established and become functional. It should be realized, however, that the cost of setting up these pillars and maintaining them with scarce resources is a considerable challenge. Creating institutions such as an ombudsman, auditor-general and other watchdog agencies, together with the presence of an independent judiciary, an active civil society and free press, cannot be directly equated to a reduction in corruption. These pillars are more precisely the building blocks for the evolution of a democratic culture in any society that would include respect for the rule of law and hence the punishment of corrupt practices. Having all the pillars in place, as they are in South Africa, is not the same as having them all working together to fight corruption; neither does their existence guarantee a reduction in corruption. The NIS is meant to create an environment where an ethos of transparency and accountability is infused into every public institution, thus making the mere thought of corruption among officials very unlikely. To ensure that each pillar is fully functional with adequate resources is a separate challenge for developing countries and one which, in terms of the NIS design, would ordinarily require substantial assistance from donor partners. It is difficult to locate any country in the developing world where the NIS has been completely adopted, effectively implemented and continuously sustained. The fundamental flaw with the NIS from a costs point of view is its reliance on 'international actors' for the implementation of its principles. To accept that corruption has increased and to believe that benefits will arise from fighting it through transparent and accountable institutions seems plausible enough. To have the necessary resources at one's disposal to build and sustain these same institutions (after balancing the budget), and to ensure that they implement their mandates free of political interference is, on the other hand, an almost insurmountable challenge for the developing world.

Government budgets would be considered fully 'balanced' if a value were to be apportioned to each item being costed in terms of how it ranks on a national scale of priorities.[7] Yet this is something that rarely happens because the way in which budgetary allocations are made is usually characterized by political bargaining and trade-offs, between and within ministries and departments. Failure to secure adequate funding for fighting corruption may have as much to do with the ability of an individual minister, or head of department, to negotiate the relevant increases or to make a strong enough case for the allocation of new resources. It is worth mentioning that despite strong pleas from the South African Public Service Commission (PSC), only £35,000 in additional funds was secured for the country's new National Anti-Corruption Hotline in September 2004. That the introduction of the hotline was in part an attempt to reduce the cost of having multiple anti-corruption hotlines throughout the public service mattered little to the state treasury officials who were empowered to advise on such matters. After Cabinet had taken a decision in August 2004 that government should play the leading role in organizing the second National Anti-Corruption Summit, the PSC was left in no doubt that no amount of funding for this purpose would be made available from the national purse. A budget of over £70,000 was projected for this event to be held and, as was the norm, letters were subsequently sent out by the PSC requesting technical assistance from its donor partners, as it had done for the first summit in 1999. One cannot escape the conclusion that to the present government in South Africa the *value* of fighting corruption is greatly inferior to a range of other competing values. Those higher priority values might include the hosting of the Pan-African Parliament, providing a private jet for the president's air travel, budgeting millions of rand for the celebrations of South Africa's ten years of democracy (held in 2004), and engaging in endless peace initiatives in strife-torn parts of Africa. Purely in terms of cost, the balance is not in favour of increased spending to fight corruption when it is pitted against these more 'important' matters. If corruption were a priority, despite the claims of national government, it would be subjected to a cost calculation and included as a line item in the budgetary allocation. Public perceptions confirm that corruption is on the increase. Though, from available evidence, increased spending to alleviate the effects of such corruption, with its attendant benefits, has not been seriously contemplated, this strategic option remains available to the South African government at any given time.

More pay, no gain

It is possible to argue that spending more on containing corruption can indirectly reduce the attendant benefits to society, and that such 'corruption control makes government ineffective' in the long term.[8] Some examples will suffice to illustrate this point further.

Employment laws

If one looks at the matter of employment reforms in the public sector, one can see that a range of initiatives have been introduced to ensure that a far more professional standard of service is offered to the public by qualified personnel who are free of corrupt intentions. But there is a downside to such reforms as well. In the public sector, it is extremely difficult to dismiss, punish or transfer a manager for poor performance because of the plethora of rules and regulations that have been introduced for employee protection. The steps to be followed are quite complex to adhere to correctly unless one is trained in the application of legislation governing labour relations. To employ a manager to fill a vacancy takes an inordinate amount of time that involves drafting a tediously 'correct' notice for advertisement in the print media (which should include standard clauses concerning gender and equal opportunity), allowing time for applicants to respond, and specifying the minimum requirements attached to the vacancy, allowing further for time to process the applications, short-listing, interviewing, offering the selected candidate the position, negotiating salary and other conditions, and finally receiving a written response from the appointee after a specified time that the offer of employment has been accepted. All of these steps have to be *strictly* adhered to so as to prevent any grievances being launched by unsuccessful candidates, as the bureaucracy will usually remind us.

Unlike the private sector, where 'head-hunting' a suitable candidate at short notice for a managerial position is the norm, the public sector is quite disadvantaged by the amount of time that must elapse for each step of the hiring process to take its course. Worse still, a vacancy must usually be subjected to a 'job evaluation' before it is advertised, and in some cases psychological testing and the obtainment of security clearance are required before the desired candidate is hired. To effect an internal transfer or promotion, which would reduce the impact of the bureaucratic nightmare, and allow for proper matchmaking of person to position, requires an even more complex procedure. To employ public officials on the basis of competency, efficiency and motivation in the absence of the above intruding requirements is virtually impossible. Yet these same requirements have mostly been introduced ostensibly to prevent corruption in the form of nepotism and patronage from taking place. Some may find the efficacy of these measures to be questionable. Most senior civil service positions must first be advertised in the media (at considerable expense) before being filled, though ministers are known to choose their own senior officials on the basis of personal relationships and party loyalty, rather than merit. The savings that might be made by departments in foregoing this requirement alone would run into thousands of pounds. In other words, it is common knowledge that patronage does take place, and if it is to continue, it would be cost-effective to allow ministers, and their senior staff (who would be responsible for appointing lower-ranked officials), the necessary latitude or 'grease' to keep the wheels of government turning.

Some might argue that a trusted colleague in a key post can make a lot of difference, and so patronage should be allowed, provided it does not become excessive and out of control. Others might say that it is already present in the public sector, and always has been, and that less time and money should be spent worrying about it, let alone on adopting measures to guard against it.

Financial disclosure

When business ethics are introduced into the public sector to help prevent corruption one of the first things that is introduced is usually a financial disclosure framework. Completion of financial disclosure forms is meant to promote transparency about potential conflicts of interest. However, such a form can also be a licence for the official to 'protect' his or her private interests by being open about them, since it is not mandatory to detect and punish such conflicts of interest if they exist. The definition of corruption has certainly expanded to the point that the right to privacy has been severely undermined by parliamentarians having to report the business interests of their spouses. All financial investments in bonds, trusts, annuities and bank accounts are usually meant to be reported, such that one's net financial worth and collective business interests become an open secret. Information of this nature is private, but having to report it to certain government officials (some of whom might be colleagues) puts a manager's private interests at high risk of exposure and manipulation. Such a financial disclosure requirement will actually deter qualified but wealthy applicants, for example 'turnaround' executives from the private sector (i.e. those specifically engaged to change the fortunes of a failing company), from seeking public service jobs. This may partially explain why, despite the improved managerial salary packages, the flow of personnel is usually in one direction only, namely from the public to the private sector.

The threat of punishment for not submitting one's financial disclosure form could be seen as a way of treating public officials like prisoners on probation in the criminal justice system. Rather than relying on personal integrity, a sense of public duty and norms of the profession, ethics rules such as those embodied in a code of conduct for the civil service would seem to invoke an atmosphere of control, surveillance and investigation. The morale of civil servants inevitably suffers if their guiding motto is to get through the day without being caught, and if they are seen as potential criminals seeking opportunities for personal enrichment at every turn rather than as loyal officials making sacrifices in the public interest. Financial disclosure and ethics rules, therefore, while introduced (at a cost) to immediately prevent forms of corrupt practices, can have a negative effect, and may actually produce fewer benefits in the long term than might otherwise be the case.

Whistle-blowing

Another example would be the downside of whistle-blowing (irrespective of motive, the act of reporting perceived or alleged misconduct in an organization to an internal or external authority), which can increase the cost of fighting corruption without necessarily bringing about a reduction in corruption levels. Whistle-blowing tends to produce costs both for the whistle-blower and the employer that are often underestimated. Furthermore, some cases of whistle-blowing originate from allegedly incompetent individuals who falsely claim protection under the relevant legislation in order to stave off pending disciplinary action against them. Protected whistle-blowers acting with questionable intent can legally hold on to their jobs for as long as their cases are being resolved, and can also harass their supervisors and cause mayhem in the organization before they eventually depart.

An important consideration is the extent to which whistle-blowing serves to undermine the authority structures and chain of command within a department. If someone successfully blows the whistle on a colleague, it becomes quite difficult for a supervisor to exercise discipline over the whistle-blower without inviting the allegation that such discipline is a form of reprisal and retaliation. Managers will be persuaded to proceed with utmost caution in enforcing discipline if the threat that their actions will be constantly referred to external agencies looms too large. A good manager can easily have his or her reputation tarnished by a whistle-blower with ulterior motives, and may lose face and authority if the same whistle-blower continues in his or her employment under protection. Sometimes the introduction of whistle-blowing legislation can have the effect of turning all employees in government into investigators and activists in uncovering corruption. Since it is an offence to bear witness to corrupt activities and keep silent about it, all civil servants are supposed to be constantly on the lookout for misdemeanours by colleagues, lest it be proven that they themselves are an accessory to the act.

Procurement procedures

The line of argument that increasing the money spent on combating corruption can actually lead to a reduction in benefits may also be extended to procurement practices (the full range of activities related to the acquisition of goods and services). In most public sector contexts of the developing world, there have been attempts to reform procurement procedures at minimal cost in order to minimize corruption. The discretion of the project manager in choosing the most appropriate contractor gets weighed down by new regulations, such that contractors get into a position of exercising a stronger influence on the bidding process than before. If a company enters the public sector bidding process with the lowest price, and has the necessary 'empowerment' credentials (usually along race or gender lines), the possibility of being granted the tender is greatly enhanced. The project manager's ability to obtain goods and services of a superior quality may well be sacrificed if contracts are awarded with little attention being given to a company's performance credentials. The emphasis on price creates a strong incentive for all bidding companies to know what their rival bidders' prices are, thus indirectly encouraging the bribery of government officials involved in the project.

A further incentive for corruption arises through 'fronting', where companies are forced to seek innovative ways of showing their empowerment credentials (even if these do not de facto exist) in order to compete favourably. If shoddy workmanship has resulted from poor public works contracting, in some housing developments for example, a situation is created where other poorly performing companies (such as plumbers and electricians who claim to be able to correct the shoddy work) are encouraged to enter the fray and mislead government by quoting low prices and lying about their own empowerment credentials. Companies with good reputations for professional service, on the other hand, become cynical and are discouraged from bidding for government contracts when they see the abuse. This is apart from the issues of massive red tape and slow payments that characterize business transactions in the public sector generally. Competition suffers as the lowest bidder is not always the one who will get the job done best. Another complicating factor is the need to ensure that companies listed on a government's debarment register (if it exists) are not awarded contracts, thus creating an extra layer of bureaucratic procedures to be followed at additional cost and time.

Costs and benefits

The problem with attempts at corruption control, which include whistle-blowing, procurement procedure improvements and public employment reforms, as discussed, is the absence of a correlation between the introduction of such measures and a reduction in corruption. While one may tacitly accept the need for such interventions at whatever cost, it is more difficult to establish their effectiveness in causing corruption to decline either slowly or rapidly. We have noted that in some cases new opportunities for corruption will inadvertently be created in trying to control corruption. Solutions to one set of problems merely create another set of problems: by making it difficult to act corruptly, it becomes more difficult to control corruption. The question that must be asked is whether by being obsessive about rules and regulations for monitoring and policing public conduct, government has become less efficient and effective by incurring a range of non-monetary costs like declining staff morale, strategic fatigue, a managerial psychosis of fear, reluctance to take risks, lack of organizational flexibility and poor responsiveness to public demands. It is little wonder that many public managers are happy to account for their conformity to rules rather than their attainment of goals.

The cost of corruption control is only likely to increase as levels of corruption decrease. Government would be wise to quantify its costs and include them within the budgetary framework, creating a value for money chain that ensures benefits to society and to government itself, before embarking on a battery of anti-corruption measures. Costs must not exceed benefits and everything should be done to ensure that less costly strategies that can work equally effectively are not overlooked. If the original reasons for the creation of certain anti-corruption measures have dissipated, there is no point in retaining them. However, because such information is not easily obtainable, and because measuring corruption itself is so problematic, it becomes difficult to know whether or not the methods employed to fight corruption are the most effective.

Pay less and gain more

The discussion so far might have created the bleak impression that fighting corruption is a wasteful exercise that involves spending taxpayers' money for few immediate benefits. Some would conclude that the amount of corruption will continue to increase and that government controls will achieve little by way of a reduction. We first noted that increased corruption results in high levels of costs in order to control it. Despite the benefits that can result from this level of spending, many governments seem reluctant or simply unable to produce budgets that can cover these costs. When costs increase and benefits get reduced, we may wonder if governments are unwittingly spending money without due regard to the negative long-term effects. This is not to imply that governments should ignore corruption (something we discounted earlier), but that a bureaucratic preoccupation with regulation and control can have detrimental effects and reduce the overall benefits of fighting corruption. It is something to be borne in mind at all times by activists engaged in confronting governments about the actions they may or may not take against corruption.

The need for a single anti-corruption agency

All is not doom and gloom, however, if another scenario – that of spending less and achieving more – is envisaged. As far-fetched as it may sound, it is possible to decrease the costs of fighting corruption and still derive some benefits from doing so. This may be described as a practical policy option that involves government reducing its 'budget' for controlling corruption and redirecting its resources towards the establishment of a single anti-corruption agency led by a 'graft buster' or anti-corruption 'champion'. This is an option that is most highly recommended for the attention of the public sector in countries hoping to achieve a *rational balance* (where the basic steps are followed with particular attention to costs and impact) in controlling the costs and benefits of fighting corruption.

It is imperative that any government policy intervention is preceded by the development of a thorough understanding of the workings of relevant state department(s) and of the respective policy programmes or systems that need changing. Alternative courses of action must be put forward for consideration by multiple actors (within the public and private sectors, and civil society). The consequences of each option will then need to be explored before implementation, as, of course, do the costs and benefits. The process of deciding on a certain policy direction should involve wide stakeholder participation, so that public reaction to it is to some degree predictable. The capacity of the country and its infrastructure should also be assessed to ensure that proper implementation will follow. Furthermore, it is a recipe for failure when governments seek to appease public sentiment by adopting policies without measuring the costs of implementation against budgetary constraints. As we noted at the outset, this will require clarification of values, principles and priorities, so that there is overall consistency in what government is attempting for the country as a whole. The precise role of the relevant department(s), minister(s), and other officials must be clearly spelt out to avoid duplication, and timeframes must be set within which to monitor and evaluate implementation. It is a fallacy to believe that good intentions will result in effective policies, hence the need for the above steps to be carefully adhered to (almost as a rule) if a country is to benefit from following proper policy procedures.

Unfortunately, a pattern emerges where a number of these steps are specifically mentioned for attention, but others are ignored as the public sector 'muddles' its way through corruption. If policy process is to be observed as it should, involving wide stakeholder participation, serious consideration should be given to the need for a feasibility study (involving cost-benefit analysis, usually done at the expense of a great deal of time and cost) to determine the extent of corruption in any given country and the possible alternative courses of action that should inform policy development. This is at least one point where, once again, the policy process on fighting corruption can begin.

Fighting corruption is as much about changing public perceptions as it is about reducing the actual levels of corruption, whether these can be measured or not. Robert Klitgaard's 'framework for policymakers' offers 'real examples' of how corruption has been successfully controlled through the engagement of what we may call 'graft busters'.[9] In Hong Kong's successful fight against corruption, Jack Cater, the first person to head the Independent Commission Against Corruption, stands out for the leadership he provided in bringing the corrupt to court. The success in the Philippines during the 1970s in bringing tax corruption under control cannot be understood without appreciating the key role played by Justice Plana.

Whether the corruption 'clean-up' is in La Paz, Bolivia (Mayor Ronald MacLean Abaroa), Tanzania (Justice Warioba) or South Africa (Judge Willem Heath), the role played by the 'graft busters' who champion the cause and give the struggle against corruption the necessary public profile should not escape us. In South Africa's case, Willem Heath is still most highly regarded throughout the world for his work when, as a judge, he was appointed by then President Mandela to head the Special Investigating Unit. Though it remains a challenge to evaluate the net effect of his efforts to recover state assets and prevent further corruption, his constant engagement with the public (through the media) was a major boost for public confidence in government's attempts to control corruption. Such public interaction was given a very high priority by the ICAC as well and helps explain why the media is an intrinsic pillar of integrity in the fight against corruption anywhere. Role models, which is what the 'graft busters' are, seem to exact the highest respect from the citizenry, and it is important for such leaders to be strategically positioned, and empowered, to lead the fight against corruption. But this cannot happen if the mandate to tackle corruption is shared among an array of organizations. With the removal of Willem Heath from office, and his 'firing' as a judge by President Mbeki in 2004, South Africa lost its champion, and no one has since been put forward to assume that role.

There is a strong case to be made for the establishment of a single anti-corruption agency, one that will be fully independent, adequately resourced and headed by a leader of the highest integrity. Only the broad outlines for such an effort can be mentioned here, but it certainly contrasts with the multi-agency approach often advocated by political leaders who fear devolution of power. One of the leading Asian scholars on good governance, Jon Quah, observes that in Asia the 'first pattern of corruption control is the simplest and also least effective, as it consists of anti-corruption laws that are not implemented by a specialized anti-corruption agency'.[10] The second pattern of having anti-corruption laws with multiple agencies, like the practice in India and the Philippines, is equally ineffective, but 'the third pattern of using an independent anti-corruption agency to implement the anti-corruption laws impartially', which is still the case in Hong Kong and Singapore, is most effective.[11] In South Africa's 'muddled' efforts to control corruption, a new comprehensive law has been enacted with no provision made for this law to be implemented by any single department, state agency or constitutional oversight body. In this power-diluting approach, the anti-corruption initiative is arbitrarily managed by about a dozen different bodies within the public sector, raising serious questions about the efficacy of any national strategy. It is contrary to what is becoming conventional wisdom for effective good governance in controlling corruption. Creation of a single agency mandated by law to combat and prevent corruption is the most obvious strategic choice for developing nations, but for obvious reasons it is not one that will always enjoy political favour.

The introduction of anti-corruption units within departments does not help much, as they tend to function quite inefficiently with low budgets. It makes little sense to further bolster their capacity and capability above a certain minimum level. If all departments and agencies of government are to engage in fighting corruption in the midst of widespread service delivery backlogs, a situation will prevail where multiple institutions across the country will all be engaged in trying to fight corruption at the expense of other policy imperatives. To achieve the minimum standard, far more resources (financial and human) will have to be deployed for this purpose, but, as we are aware, such resources are ordinarily not available. Even if existing budgets are depleted, it may be more cost-effective if all such anti-corruption units are closed down, and their resources transferred to a central agency. Such a single centralized operation should then assume all the anti-corruption functions previously exercised by this plethora of bodies and departmental units. Many such agencies were brought into existence with specifically designated functions other than fighting corruption and should, for this reason, continue operating. A new independent anti-corruption organization, established along the lines of Hong Kong's ICAC, but with a much smaller budget, will nonetheless provide an important and added boost to the confidence of the nation and foreign investors about government's will to clamp down on corruption. It will send a positive signal to the entire world that such a government is serious about protecting its hard-fought gains in democracy, justice and national reconciliation. The appointment of an individual with impeccable credentials to lead such a new initiative will be a critical decision, as such a person must operate without fear or favour, but enjoy the respect and admiration of all. Perception matters, whether government accepts that or not, and the identification of 'graft busters' is a matter deserving urgent attention to advance the struggle against corruption.

Of course, if there is to be a rationalization of the anti-corruption functions exercised by many role-players in the public sector, spending on anti-corruption projects will then be undertaken by a single agency whose work should not be frustrated by a less than *adequate* budget. The state treasury may find it difficult to secure new allocations of revenue for such a new agency. Parliament, which has final oversight over the national budget, must ensure that the country is not robbed of the necessary resources to control something that is a menace to society and so detrimental to the public interest. This will probably lead to a situation where the costs of fighting corruption are reduced (initially at least, as all other anti-corruption projects will either be amalgamated with the new agency or closed down), possibly resulting in increased benefits to society (at least in terms of public perception and investor confidence). It is beyond the scope of our immediate interest to establish on a scientific basis that such a single agency will in fact produce such benefits, make government's work against corruption more effective, and be more efficient than a multi-agency approach. However, it is clear that the implementation of a national strategy against corruption will be severely compromised by a lack of sufficient resources. The 'best practice' of Hong Kong, on the one hand, and the failure of the multi-agency approach in Asia on the other, both strongly suggest the need for developing countries to reconsider their options in fighting corruption. Costs must as a rule not exceed benefits, but neither should the pursuit of 'zero tolerance at whatever cost' towards corruption render government ineffective. The need for a *rational balance* to be sought where the basic steps of policy process are followed with particular attention to costs and impact is therefore the impinging challenge if corruption is to be fought effectively. We have made a strong case for public officials to reconsider budgeting for the costs of fighting corruption in order to achieve a greater impact.

Fighting corruption: an end in itself

It is a positive expression of a country's desire to develop economically when it seeks to combat and prevent corruption but, through lack of adequate resources, the efficacy of such an effort cannot be assured. While some additional spending by government on anti-corruption initiatives might bring in some benefits, as we have tried to show, it is far from clear that national government (and the tax-payer as a result) is not the loser when money spent on solving one set of problems leads to further bureaucratization and more costs. The view advocated here is that young democratic nations would be better served by an independent single agency within their public sector which will be dedicated to fighting corruption alone and led by a person of sound integrity. This is contrary to the options recommended by the United Nations, where the multi-agency approach is recognized as beneficial and useful for the fight against corruption to be better managed. Our emphasis has been to show that, in order to maximize its impact, the task of fighting corruption anywhere will need to be regarded as a fiscal end within the national budgetary framework. Failure to undertake such reform of the national strategy on corruption leaves open the question of whether political rhetoric against corruption is sufficiently matched by a commitment of re-sources. Heavy reliance on donor support to fund what should be a national priority, particularly for a developing country, is unlikely to be sustainable over the long term. Hence the need to include the costs of fighting corruption as a standard line item in the expend-iture framework of the state treasury. The process of calculating such costs is best facilitated by rationalizing the multiple units already involved in fighting corruption (where they may exist) and creating a single fully resourced organization instead. This, of course, must be preceded by a policy shift in perception by a national government about the continuing value of addressing the problem of corruption.

Part 3

CONFRONTING CORRUPTION

5

A South African case study

The previous chapters of this book might have sounded somewhat academic to those with an appetite for real life situations or a case study approach to understanding how corruption 'lives'. With no end to corruption in sight, its obfuscating character causes it to be covered up one day or exposed the next, banished from one context but exported to another, condemned by all yet 'allowed' when circumstances become extraordinary. The 1990s, after the fall of the Berlin Wall, witnessed a surge in the replacement of previously authoritarian regimes throughout the world by democratic governments. Eastern Europe was in many ways the melting pot as one country after another began to shake off the dust of decades of communist rule and welcome the harbingers of global capitalism. Much further south, in Africa, Nelson Mandela had been released in 1990 after spending 27 years in prison. He was on his way to becoming South Africa's first democratically elected president. How would he cope with the centuries of underdevelopment that his people were subjected to and how would his country take its place on a continent notorious for the proliferation of corrupt practices? More than a decade after he vacated office, it is possible to reflect with the benefit of hindsight on how he coped with corruption as a salutary lesson for those who imagine that it can be wished away. The story of how Mandela dealt with corruption is told here in considerable detail as it has never been told before. But more than that, it brings us back to the problem of corruption as we understand it – that we can never say never to its uninviting presence at the best of times. That Mandela remains a moral leader held in the highest esteem by people around the world cannot be doubted; he is the same man who presided over a government that took up the task of confronting corruption quite seriously. If he succeeded, it was because of his own commitment; if he failed, as some might say he did, it could be attributed to those who followed in his footsteps.

Apartheid as corruption

How did corruption manifest itself in a developing country like South Africa before 1994, when there was no collective effort or governmental strategy to bring it under control? When Mandela came to power he inherited a situation where there was little legislation to fight corruption; this became a considerable problem for the new democratic government. Not many have given this matter much attention, yet we cannot advance to a deeper understanding of the issues involved if we are treated to reckless observations such as those of one writer who blames South Africa's transition to democracy under Mandela for the 'decline of morals and values to such a magnitude that corruption, maladministration, and financial mismanagement have become major issues tainting the public sector'.[1] A good starting point might rather be to note the observation of someone who has given the fight against corruption some attention. Before 1994, when South Africa made its transition to a democratic government, the Speaker of the National Parliament, Frene Ginwala, observed in a keynote address to the Africa Leadership Forum that this apartheid legacy was characterized by:

> a society that was organized to provide everything for a racial minority regardless of the consequences to whoever was affected; it was managed by a secret society of brothers who furthered their objectives through strategies devised in secret; to achieve their objectives they placed their brother members in all positions of influence and power – civil servants, and in politics, in state institutions and parastatals [public utility companies], in the army, and the police; inside the country human rights were violated . . . wars and civil strife were fermented; the laws of many countries were violated by breaking sanctions – and in the process enormous so-called commissions were paid to leaders or officials, to obtain the sanctioned good, especially oil and arms. But also in the course of trade in other goods – certificates of origin, and user certificates, ship manifests and custom declarations were falsified and public records were corrupted.[2]

Ginwala's summary of the nature of political corruption before 1994, though not based on factual evidence, would appear to dovetail with the commonly held perception that South Africa experienced corruption in various forms and sizes during the apartheid years. The real extent of such corruption would be extremely difficult to quantify, but its peculiar features and routine characteristics were known.

Corruption by definition bears no respect for the unique nature of any political system, but the forms it takes can certainly be influenced by the quality of democracy that a society's citizens are exposed to at any given time. Apartheid, understood as a policy of racial exclusion and economic oppression, seems to have carefully defined the peculiar shape and forms that corruption assumed in South Africa, as we shall see.

'Arguably,' says political scientist Tom Lodge, 'a bureaucracy which was deliberately used as an instrument to foster the social and economic fortunes of one ethnically defined group had at least a form of transactive corruption built into its functioning' from 1948 when the predominantly Afrikaner-supported National Party took political power.[3] This party was to dominate South African politics until 1994, forming in the process a series of repressive governments all upholding the supreme interests of Afrikaner nationalism, but where corruption as *personal gain* arising from individualized relationships was probably minimal.[4] It has also been argued that by the 1970s civil servants had 'little opportunity to use patronage and the conferment of financial benefits for the achievement of improper objectives' in a climate of tight monetary controls and strict financial discipline.[5] Lodge confirms this finding by indicating that the reports of the Auditor-General for the 1950s and 1960s show evidence of a relatively small number of misdemeanours, mostly confined to the Post Office, where minor sums of money would have been misused. During these years it might be safe to conclude that the most common form of overt corruption was nepotism, where administrative posts in government departments and credit allocations for agricultural farming would be reserved for National Party supporters.[6] But with the pressures of modernization, and the need to justify apartheid, the situation was to change dramatically from the late 1970s onwards. According to one commentator, as the economy stagnated, 'the country seems to have shifted dramatically from a low corruption–high growth to a high corruption–low growth scenario'.[7]

One of the important reasons why the National Party governments were able to indulge in corrupt activities to an extraordinary extent was their development of a political strategy called 'total onslaught'. Apartheid in this scheme, as opposition politician Alex Boraine noted, was 'presented not as an indefensible race policy but as engaged in a noble struggle against evil forces of international atheistic communism'.[8] This meant that all the draconian actions of government, including its infringement of civil liberties, regular abuse of state power, and corrupt practices, were 'excusable' in pursuit of this strategy. Feeling the impact of diplomatic isolation, and the development of a security threat around its borders, the government began secretly investing millions of rand into buying political influence at home and abroad. The Department of Information was designated to channel such funds into buying newspapers, bribing journalists, and engaging in covert operations, among other secret projects. For example, £1 million was loaned to businessman Louis Luyt to start the *Citizen* newspaper, but most of this money ended up being invested in the bank accounts of his private companies.[9] The private sector was mostly dominated by white-owned companies that enjoyed a fair measure of protection and secrecy, and with the help of the state, penetrated international markets despite the sanctions in force against South Africa at the time. Thus, though large business corporations operating in the country might have voiced their objections to apartheid, they benefited by and large by being 'an accomplice of a corrupt system of governance'.[10]

In 1978 the corrupt practices of the Department of Information were disclosed and, more dramatically, individuals who had personally enriched themselves were exposed. The 'Information Scandal', as it became known, had siphoned off over £4 million and was conducted in the absence of parliamentary oversight. The mastermind behind this whole undertaking, and one of its main benefactors, was a senior government official, Eschel Rhoodie, whose 927-page account of its strategic operations differed radically from that of the official Erasmus Commission that investigated the matter. Rhoodie expressed his disgust at the 'cover-up' that ensued, claiming that 'the real Information Scandal' must be laid at the feet of those 'Members of Parliament who have accepted, supported, and voted for the passage of legislation the past decade, notably the past few years, which provided the government with protective measures that exceeded the boundaries of natural justice, common sense, and the real requirements of the State'.[11] The biggest casualties in the whole debacle were Prime Minister John Vorster, who was forced to vacate office, and Information Minister Connie Mulder, who, for all his efforts, lost the race to become the new prime minister to his defence counterpart, P. W. Botha. Although certain sections of the media, the Auditor-General, and Mr Justice Anton Mostert eschewed their watchdog role throughout the scandal, one report suggests that Mostert qualifies as South Africa's first 'whistle-blower' for having resisted political interference and for upholding the independence of the judiciary. He ignored P. W. Botha's request to withhold from the media information related to the scandal.[12]

Corruption was also clearly rampant in the Department of Development Aid, which channelled state funds into the creation and maintenance of the so-called homeland states or bantustans (vast tracts of land set aside for occupation by blacks under the administration of government-appointed leaders). The commission led by Mr Justice Pickard that investigated this department concluded that 'theft, dishonesty, corruption, fraud, negligence, and unauthorized activities resulted in huge losses. It most certainly ran into many millions, if not billions.'[13] The responsible Cabinet minister, Gerrit Viljoen, saw no reason to resign, claiming that such a step was not customary in South Africa. The Department of Defence was equally notorious for engaging in clandestine activities both at home and abroad, sections of its budget allocation being beyond public scrutiny. Funds used for political propaganda were sometimes 'hidden' in its cost structure as it secretly also began producing sophisticated small arms for illegal sale on the open market. The role of South African soldiers in fuelling the war in Angola and their involvement in ivory smuggling and drug trafficking were further breeding grounds for corruption, as were the millions of pounds spent by government to develop a strategic fuel reserve to offset the country's dwindling oil reserves.[14] The Department of Education and Training was also the subject of an inquiry in 1988 after repeated reports of corruption had appeared in the media. The Van den Heever Commission, set up to investigate alleged irregularities, produced three volumes of evidence of extensive fraud, kickbacks, bribery, nepotism and poor accountability to prove the corruption suspicions.

Case study: Corrupting crimes of apartheid

If our interest in the subject of apartheid-era corruption is limited to learning more about our history as a nation, then we will benefit, at the very least, from the wisdom of hindsight. However, this could also represent a missed opportunity, for as the past slips away so too do the perpetrators and witnesses of such crimes. Evidence of these crimes will be further erased over time and money stolen will continue to enrich the beneficiaries of corruption. In taking this path, we choose to close the book on the past. Such a decision will not threaten the South African elite and will no doubt be welcomed by many. It will, however, probably always haunt us as a society. If billions of rand were stolen, this path means they will not be made available to be used for reconstruction and development. When we see the patterns of old replicate themselves in our democratic society, we will also have to admit that we have chosen not to fundamentally break these cycles.

If we choose to forthrightly engage with the past, head on, through initial calls for more information and eventually criminal investigations, resourced by the state, we will have chosen a risky option but one which may reward us in many ways. It could help in seeing money returned to the country and long-denied justice being done. Many obstacles will have to be negotiated in the process: it cannot become a witch-hunt but should be a process owned by all South Africans. It should not detract from current investigations but should rather seek to ensure that the country's anti-corruption efforts are bolstered. It would require a change in the law, as commercial crimes 'age' after 20 years. If carefully managed, it could represent an important step in healing the divides that continue to scar this land. If not correctly handled, it could also entrench divisions within society, alienate private capital and impact negatively on South African society. However, if this is seen as a process, such obstacles could be negotiated step by step.

(Extract from Hennie van Vuuren, *Apartheid Grand Corruption: Assessing the scale of Crimes of Profit in South Africa from 1976 to 1994*, Pretoria: Institute for Security Studies, 2006, pp. 86–7.)

Of course, it could be argued that much of the corruption prevalent during the apartheid years was in the 'public interest', insofar as the public that mattered was the white electorate. But as was reported in the media, much of the corrupt behaviour of the time brought immense personal benefits to those found guilty by the commission and those who were cleared of wrongdoing.[15] Homeland leaders were best off: they received millions of pounds to develop their 'independent' states and thus maintain the apartheid system, much of these funds, however, being used to enrich themselves and their friends and families. But this mattered little to the government of the day.[16] Many forms of corruption were permitted so long as the grand design of apartheid ideology remained intact.

Against this background, it would be misleading to assume that the majority of the citizens, being excluded from the political franchise, chose to be moral men and women in an immoral society. The opposite was true. The liberation movement that was sweeping the country and preparing itself for rule in the foreseeable future had decided that South Africa should be turned into an ungovernable country in order to hasten the demise of apartheid. A culture militating against respect for the rule of law was therefore encouraged. With Mandela's accession to power, the very people who had suffered under a repressive political system and were forced into acts of civil disobedience, sometimes corruption, in order to survive and 'beat the system' were required overnight to become champions of democracy and respect the rule of law. Apartheid may have constituted grand-scale corruption, but it also invited a culture of lawlessness to evolve, making the task of confronting corruption by the Mandela government much more complex, as we shall see.

New corruption

Apartheid South Africa, up to the early 1990s and especially through its bantustan homelands policy, offered a unique environment for certain forms of corrupt practices to flourish because of inadequate checks and controls. But what about the country after Mandela took office in 1994? This was obviously the most significant year in the history of South Africa thus far, as the country made its transition from apartheid to democracy under Mandela's leadership. The years of democratic rule since 1994, however, have also ushered in new and far more sophisticated forms and types of corruption than ever seen before in South Africa, much to the dismay of the law enforcement agencies who were little prepared for such a development. Organized crime made increasing gains through its profligate activities, as a culture of lawlessness appeared to take root in South African society, thus making it an even more fertile ground for corruption to succeed.

If it is true that corruption has been on the increase since 1994, equally true is the determination of society, particularly the national government, to take steps to remedy the situation. This determination was initially expressed more at the rhetorical than the practical level, with little or no thought given to the matter of the costs and benefits of fighting corruption. Yet when President Mandela began making way for a successor, after five years in office, the first attempts to set forth a plan for a national anti-corruption strategy began to take shape within government. This involved a series of consultations with various stakeholders, inside and outside the public sector, and often with international partners as well, and the introduction of a range of measures that culminated in the adoption of new legislation in 2003 to outlaw corruption in most of its overt forms.

Policy shift

To appreciate the dynamics of a transition to democracy a brief overview of the changing policy environment and the ways in which policy shifts were effected will now be provided. The task of fighting corruption was obviously one that signalled a radical departure from the policies pursued prior to 1994, hence the need to articulate some of the contributing factors that caused such a policy adjustment. The development of the national strategy against corruption took place in various phases, beginning with a series of discussions at Cabinet level and the release of a report that provided guidelines for strategic action. This was followed by a national public sector consultation at which a national agenda or action plan to fight corruption began to emerge in anticipation of the more representative national summit that was held later. The national strategy, which served as the basis for the national government's anti-corruption efforts, was agreed upon at the next phase when the national summit was held, with then Deputy President Thabo Mbeki playing a decisive role in proceedings. The summit called for the establishment of a national cross-sectoral body that would 'manage' the anti-corruption programme. The formal launch of this National Anti-Corruption Forum (NACF) marked the final phase in the process of building 'national consensus' to fight corruption and therefore merits further consideration.

The existence of the apartheid state prior to 1994 contributed to the creation of a conducive environment for corruption to flourish, often in entrenched and disguised form. The harsh policies pursued by the former government were greatly detrimental to the country and its citizens, hence the need for rapid and radical change with the transition to democracy. The seismic shifts in policy that were to be the hallmark of the first democratic government were not initiated in a vacuum following textbook Western-style models but rather through particular policy coalitions comprising various networks and communities. While the problem of corruption was not one deserving of policy overhaul, among a host of more urgent matters such as housing, health, education, and so forth, a political stage was being set and a pattern evolving that would define how any policy was to be formulated for the foreseeable future. The 'driving forces' in this new policy thrust included 'the urgent need for delivery, the need for consistency in policies, the political culture that confers legitimacy on high political and government leadership, and the need to protect liberation gains'.[17] Political analyst Susan Booysen concludes that policymaking was as a result cast into 'a party managerial style, with the core clusters of policy actors prevailing'.[18] Before moving on to consider the nature and consequences of corruption in the democratic South Africa, it might be useful to clarify the scope and effects of policymaking through such clusters, over against the more traditional policy process. This will help explain the particular 'party managerial style' of key public sector actors who in turn played a decisive role in determining the new government's approach to fighting corruption. For it is only within a distinctive framework that departments of the state are *allowed* to be different in utilizing their unique positions, methods and consultants to restructure their policies and procedures.

Seeking policy support

The burden of overhauling policy immediately after 1994 was substantially informed by a moral imperative, for if '[a]partheid policies had been harmful and morally wrong, the new government's policies had therefore to right these wrongs, and the new policies had to be morally right'.[19] The new policy framework that emerged from the ruins of the apartheid legacy was to be called the 'Reconstruction and Development Programme' (RDP). This was a comprehensive governmental initiative for the amelioration of the socio-economic conditions of all citizens, especially blacks, and sought 'to eradicate imbalances and gross injustices of the past' and 'create the necessary conditions for a stable and viable democratic South African state'.[20] To replace the old authoritarian, regulatory and unaccountable administration, the RDP sought to create the basis for an open, accountable and people-oriented approach in all government business. Civil society would henceforth become an active player in policymaking. Draft policy documents were published to encourage public response, while conferences and workshops were held regularly on specific issues. Public hearings and public participation in parliamentary briefings were also held, while a significant development was the formation of forums to provide a context within which to achieve consensus on key policy matters such as the economy, labour, water, gender and, later, corruption itself.

The RDP was closely aligned to the election manifesto of the ruling African National Congress (ANC)-dominated government, and had apparently been informed by 'neo-Keynesian assumptions and policy prescriptions, which had lost favour in the World Bank and IMF'.[21] For a while though, South Africa's peaceful transition to democracy had given it the moral right to be different, and the extensive use of consultative and participatory modes of governance gave its policy experiments legitimacy among most of the citizenry and the international community as well.

By 1996, however, policy shifts were in the making with the closure of the RDP office during the Mandela presidency and the adoption of a new Growth, Employment and Redistribution (GEAR) policy framework. This was in essence an economic plan entailing the containment of state expenditure, lower inflation, privatization, lower fiscal deficits, and increased foreign investment devised by elitist economists of the World Bank, the Department of Finance and the Universities of Cape Town and Stellenbosch.[22] The 'economic exceptionalism' permitted under the RDP seemed over, as South Africa now had to catch up with the new world economic order on terms that were not of its own making. But GEAR largely failed to deliver economic growth, reduce unemployment, or improve the social conditions of the masses and was severely criticized by the Congress of South African Trade Unions (COSATU) and the South African Communist Party (SACP), both alliance partners of the ruling ANC party.[23] Some commentators believe that this failure forced the ANC to 'reintroduce the RDP as the government's primary development agenda',[24] while others maintained that the adoption of a neo-liberal economic policy effectively 'derailed' government's commitment to cooperative governance, as GEAR 'by its very nature does not provide for consultative process'.[25] Implementation of GEAR has produced 'mixed success and ambivalence' with policy contradictions and failure by government departments to act decisively on corruption, capital wastage, the quality of administration, and crime.[26] After the second democratic election of 1999, with Mandela no longer at the helm, the policy challenge shifted from formulation to implementation. There were fewer opportunities for wide stakeholder participation, and 'consultation was primarily based on bureaucratic and political interpretation'.[27] Booysen also observes that 'when deadlines for policy delivery became pressing', there was 'evidence of lip service' being paid to policy consultation.[28] The co-operative governance mode of managing policy change was maintained, but a growing divide was also becoming evident among some civil society movements restless with government's pace of transformation, which was bringing little benefit to grassroots communities.

In the case of some government departments, evidence has emerged that 'there has been a pretence of widespread consultation on intended legislation and policy, but without the capacity or real intention to listen to what emerged from the consultation process, and with little interest in learning from it either'.[29] A pattern may be observed where an apparent 'confusion of policy advocacy with policy analysis' results in many within government believing their own propaganda without undertaking detailed systematic study.[30] If policy analysis is 'a structured way of thinking about choices before deciding on a particular course of action', such a method of policy formulation has been a rare phenomenon.[31] Over 300 pieces of legislation were produced between 1994 and 1999 alone, confirming the 'tendency to govern by legislation rather than sound administration'.[32] Worse, the common assumption has been that 'good intentions will automatically result in good policies', with no consideration to the enormous financial implications of implementation.[33] The 'exceedingly uncomfortable straitjackets' imposed by the demands of capital markets and international investors, in the midst of global mobility and interdependence, served to add further constraints on the policy renewal process as the rules for consultation became even more blurred.[34] Top officials in government departments, together with their policy advisors and policy consultants, who are all usually party loyalists, exerted an 'inordinate influence' in policymaking, often even greater in degree than parliament or ministers.[35] The Office of the Presidency may have been responsible for centrally directing and co-ordinating the policy process, but because of capacity constraints and lack of proper consultations, it failed to make any real impression in the policy domain.[36] With the formal establishment of Cabinet clusters (where departments of government with overlapping or related mandates devise policy after consultation at joint forums) in 1999, one would have anticipated a change in process and procedures, but evidence of such a shift is still lacking.

The secondary cluster of policy actors, after Cabinet, which would include select business allies, together with the COSATU, the SACP and parliament, had less of an influence, as policymaking remained 'executive-centric', where 'the policy and strategic positions of the top-leadership almost always prevail'.[37] Booysen's tertiary cluster of policy actors, comprising civil society, people's forums, churches and NGOs, played a role in determining needs assessment and implementation strategy, but their influence on policy was in decline. This helps explain the rise of specific policy coalitions like the Treatment Action Campaign (TAC), which successfully forced government to transcend its 'unscientific paranoia' about antiretroviral therapy to prevent mother-to-child transmission of HIV/AIDS.[38] TAC was led by an ANC member, Zachie Achmat, but their marginalization in the health policy process compelled them to take an adversarial stance against government. It is the protests of such groups, according to former World Bank vice-president Joseph Stiglitz, that are now making government officials and economists around the world think about alternatives to neo-liberal market-driven models for growth and development.[39] In an overall sense, despite the remarkable achievements of government since 1994, policy proposals have shown a 'lack of real analysis' as they tend to announce where we need to go without telling us how to get there.[40] If the resultant gap is filled by legislation, this often produces unintended and contradictory outcomes if and when it reaches the implementation stage. Both parliament and Cabinet have been reduced to playing surrogate roles of contributing to legislative debates, especially since 1999, while policy remains the preserve of a central hierarchy (comprising the president and few others). One is led to conclude therefore that the traditional rules of policymaking were being increasingly abandoned as South Africa entered the new millennium. The above overview of the policymaking process since 1994 helps in some way towards anticipating the approach that will likely be followed by the national government in fighting corruption, and the evaluation of that approach thereafter.

Measuring corruption

To what extent did corruption arise as a problem requiring government intervention? On the basis of media coverage alone, one
may be led to perceive that South Africa experienced a rapid rise in
reported incidents of corruption after 1994. As government itself
maintains no such database, most commentators have relied on investigative journalists and the print media to provide information
about corruption, since reporting such matters is in the public
interest. The New National Party (NNP), the successor to the old
National Party that ruled from 1948 to 1994, on becoming the
official opposition in the national parliament, took the bold step of
producing a public sector Corruption Barometer 1994–1998.[41] The
NNP claimed that it had the 'responsibility to expose corruption
and its causes' and owed an obligation to the voters to challenge the
ruling ANC 'to account for the threatening institutional collapse
of the public sector'.[42] The first version of the barometer, published
in 1997, excluded the Western Cape, Gauteng, Northern Cape and
North West provinces as their exposure to corruption was considered limited. The second version, published a year later, noted
that corruption cases had since doubled in the North West and that
Gauteng was now 'plagued by corruption in various departments'.[43]

The NNP's attempt to track various cases of corruption through
reports of constitutional oversight bodies (like those from the
Auditor-General or Public Protector) and newspaper articles was
beset with serious difficulties as the results of many investigations into
corrupt practices remained largely unknown, despite South Africa
becoming a transparent society. The justice system indulged itself in
lengthy delays for almost every case before it, while state departments
were not forthcoming with names and outcomes of corruption cases
that required disciplinary action. In the category of 'ghost workers'
and pension fraud scams, the information that could be procured was
minimal, especially in terms of the numbers of people involved and
the amounts of taxpayers' money stolen.[44] These problems aside,
about 4,000 cases were identified in all nine provinces and the total
amount squandered ran up to nearly £3 billion.[45] While one would
prefer to exercise caution with data provided for political consumption, the method and sources used give this work by the NNP
sufficient credibility to compare it with other similar efforts.

Using a scientifically valid instrument, the Institute for Democracy in South Africa (IDASA) initiated a series of nationally representative surveys from 1994 to 1999 on the public perception of political corruption.[46] This was an attempt to gauge the 'citizens' assessments of official corruption' and to measure levels of trust and confidence in government. Nearly half (46 per cent) of those surveyed believed that those employed in the public sector were guilty of corruption. There was a strongly held view (among 41 per cent) that corruption had been on the increase since 1994. Most corrupt practices were thought to take place in national and provincial government departments (50 per cent), with lower levels perceived at municipalities, parliament and the Office of the President. Most of the respondents in these surveys expressed their desire for greater honesty from public officials than they had been experiencing, while a third believed that these same officials were less honest than the ordinary citizens. Only a paltry 6 per cent believed that the government of the day was clean and free of corruption. The overall conclusion was obviously that South Africans held a rather negative and dismal perception of corruption in government ranks, but as perception can be misleading, further explanations were sought. One possibility raised was that the hostile and suspicious attitude was prevalent mostly among certain sub-groups, who were cynical towards black government anyway. The media could easily be the main driver in influencing public opinion, and public ignorance itself could have fuelled the cynical disposition.[47]

In 2000 another survey of the opinions of 150 'experts' (mostly managers with academic degrees and who had some direct and indirect exposure to corruption issues) on corruption was conducted by the Institute for Security Studies (ISS) to obtain new data on corruption matters and assist policymakers in devising effective strategies of combat and prevention.[48] A third of these experts knew of bribery being practised, and a further third agreed that corruption levels were the same before and after 1994. Interestingly, about half of them believed that corruption would decrease over time, while a third believed it was more likely to increase. Nearly two-thirds of those interviewed accepted that crime, security and job creation were more pressing issues for the country, though. While a large majority (83 per cent) acknowledged government's commitment to fighting corruption, 73 per cent of these experts did not believe that government resources were adequate. The Special Investigating Unit (SIU), when it was headed by Judge Willem Heath, was generally considered to be the most effective anti-corruption agency (85 per cent), followed by the Auditor-General (74 per cent) and the Public Protector (62 per cent). The two state departments most vulnerable to corrupt practices were identified as the Police Services and Home Affairs.[49] The ISS survey also established that a 'decline in morals and ethics' was one of the main causes of corruption, while greed, poverty, unemployment, mismanagement and poor controls were also responsible for its spread.[50]

In the IDASA surveys mentioned above, the Eastern Cape province was identified as ranking very high in terms of its exposure to corruption. The Public Service Accountability Monitor (PSAM), which is based in this province at Rhodes University, Grahamstown, undertook another survey in 2001 to establish the divergence of perception between government bureaucrats at the Bisho capital and the public as far as corruption was concerned.[51] PSAM were also interested in whether and how corrective action had been taken against corrupt persons. The key findings of this survey, while strictly valid only for one province out of a possible nine, can be corroborated with the NNP's barometer and the IDASA surveys, particularly with regard to the prevalence of corruption. A total of 89 per cent of the government officials surveyed in the PSAM survey felt that corruption was 'wrong and punishable' but 48 per cent found it 'not wrong' or 'wrong but understandable' to accept gifts in the performance of one's public duty. Forty-two per cent blamed democracy for the increase in corruption, 22 per cent felt corruption to be linked to low salaries, 23 per cent agreed that 'extra payments and favours' contributed to effective government, and 21 per cent of respondents were of the view that government had more important business to take care of than worry about officials earning extra money through corruption. These findings help explain why corruption in the Eastern Cape has assumed endemic proportions, and how the influence of the 'apartheid legacy of patronage and clientelism on the current administration' has taken its toll.[52] This province was, after all, the result of an amalgamation of two bantustan homelands and the eastern part of the old Cape Provincial Administration.

Corruption scandals

Cabinet decided to intervene in December 2002, when the Eastern Cape provincial administration seemed to be on the point of collapse, and sent a task team to assist in addressing the structural problems and bring corruption under control. A further national intervention into the province's Department of Education was ordered in July 2004 after it ran up a deficit of some £40 million. Even the premier of the province, his director-general and a number of his ministers were replaced after the 2004 elections in an attempt to bring about positive change. As one analyst notes, this is all too much of 'an alarming reminder that regardless of the many good policies a country such as South Africa might have to tackle graft, if unchecked by official sanction, the consequences can be disastrous'.[53]

From the information we have gathered thus far it seems possible to confirm the conclusion reached by Tom Lodge, namely that 'though old habits and dispositions may well sustain much of the existing administrative corruption, its expansion is also the consequence of change . . . the simultaneous democratization and restructuring of the South African state makes it very vulnerable to corruption'.[54] It should also be emphasized that the constitutional provisions for transparency and accountability in all government business, and the elevation of values such as access to information and just administrative action in the Bill of Rights, in defining the peculiar character of South Africa's democracy (over against its secretive past), have made corrupt behaviour more susceptible to detection even if it does not end in punishment.[55] The open nature of democracy also makes access to information previously held captive by the state less difficult to obtain, especially for investigative journalists seeking to expose such behaviour, and means that the reporting of corruption is more likely to take place without fear of reprisal.

But the reintegration of a substantial number of exiled citizens (mostly black former anti-apartheid activists returning from outside the country), usually into public office, low levels of political competition, poor and uneven economic prosperity, high levels of crime caused by an antinomian culture, and the absence of sufficient competition regulations to protect business interests have not helped. Human beings suddenly thrust into positions of power and prosperity from conditions of dire poverty are as likely to succumb to the temptations of illicit gain as those motivated by avarice. The sweeping powers of an authoritarian executive unchecked by a parliament totally dominated by a single party constitute an institutional licence to cover up corruption if and when necessary. The inheritance of a population whose majority had for hundreds of years celebrated their often illegally acquired gains in an illegitimate system of white minority rule was a recipe for the collapse of law and order. Economic growth is only possible in a stable and competitive environment, yet the moral imperatives for economic transformation made the empowerment of blacks a key priority, resulting in uncertainty and the need for further and, often, unwelcome legislation initiated by government.

A free and independent media is considered to be as pivotal to countering corruption as an independent judiciary,[56] and in South Africa since 1994 the print media at least has influenced public perceptions about high-level corruption. The country's first democratically elected Minister of Welfare, Abe Williams, was forced to resign in February 1996 from the then government of national unity in which he represented the National Party. He was prosecuted for accepting a huge bribe from a company tendering to dispense pensions and sent to jail.[57] Winnie Madikizela-Mandela, former wife of Nelson Mandela, and Deputy Minister of Arts and Culture until her dismissal in 1995, was alleged to have accepted £5,000 for helping to influence the award of low-cost housing contracts, while Housing Minister Sankie Mthembi-Mahanyele was believed to have allowed the award of a contract to a company co-owned by a close friend.[58] Early in January 1996, the *Sunday Times* reported on a parliamentary hearing into the Department of Health's award of a £1 million contract to a playwright for his 'hideously expensive, of little artistic merit, anti-Aids play, *Sarafina 2*'.[59] Regular calls were subsequently made for the Minister of Health to resign owing to the alleged wastage of taxpayers' money, cover-ups, and for misleading parliament about the matter. When the Public Protector confirmed evidence of tender violations and other irregularities in the matter, it was hoped that the president would at least reprimand the minister.[60] On the contrary, in the Cabinet reshuffle following the 1999 elections, the minister assumed the more senior Foreign Affairs portfolio.

South Africa's biggest corruption 'scandal' began to unravel in 2000 after government had signed a massive £3 billion Strategic Defence Procurement Package.[61] Contracts were entered into with numerous multinational companies for the supply of helicopters, submarines, arms and other military hardware, with particular attention given to 'offsets' and 'incentives' to justify the transactions. Numerous procedural irregularities were highlighted by the media and opposition parties in parliament, forcing government to appoint a joint investigating team to report on allegations of corruption in the whole arms deal. Some of these allegations were shown to have substance, but not enough to have influenced the entire package of transactions.[62] Numerous officials who had received gifts from some of the companies were mentioned in the report by name, while a senior official was shown to have favoured companies in which his brother, Shabir Shaik, had a stake.[63] Shaik faced a corruption trial in October 2004, and as the former financial advisor to former Deputy President Jacob Zuma (1999–2005), his case raised serious questions that Zuma himself might be implicated. The former national director of public prosecutions, Bulelani Ncguka, in any case made public that he had prima facie evidence of corruption involving the deputy president.[64] It is of further interest that none of the foreign multinational companies or their employees implicated by the media for behaving corruptly in the arms deal have faced any sanction in their respective countries.

For some years after its transition from apartheid, South Africa was therefore more at risk from the corrosive effects of corruption in the lives of its citizens, the conduct of its public servants, the behaviour of its politicians, and in the nature of its commercial transactions than ever before. The exact extent of the new forms of corruption that had taken root, in addition to the old forms, is difficult to quantify, as we saw much earlier. South Africa's rating on the Corruption Perceptions Index was by no means favourable for investor confidence.[65] In 1995 it stood at 21 out of a possible 41, and by 2003 its position had actually deteriorated in relation to countries such as Mauritius, Botswana and Tunisia. The pervasive practice of corruption, though not a new phenomenon to South Africa, had made an unwelcome blotch on the new democracy, and institutions of society, in the public sector in particular, were obliged to devise ways and means of confronting it. How this development was perceived, especially within government, and the full range of measures that were contemplated, and often enacted, to face this new corruption challenge is also of interest, and it is to this that we next turn.

Political will

With burgeoning crime levels sweeping the country after Mandela's exit from office, it was not unexpected that a National Crime Pre-

vention Strategy was devised and approved by Cabinet for implementation. In March 1997 the Cabinet ministers responsible for this
strategy established a programme committee to consider the matter
of corruption within the criminal justice system. This committee
initially included representatives of the South African Police Services
(SAPS), the Department of Correctional Services, and the Attorney-
General of the Witwatersrand. Of immediate concern to this group
was the need for a more effective system of information (which was
usually stored in files) management and greater efficiency in the
management of investigations and prosecutions. But these concerns
were not pursued as 'the committee lacked resources'.[66] In October
of that year Cabinet then requested the Minister of Justice, with the
assistance of the Minister for Public Service and Administration,
and the Minister for Provincial Government, 'to consider proposals
on the implementation at National and Provincial level of an Anti-
Corruption Campaign'. The Justice Minister at that time, Abdullah
Omar, was specifically asked to give consideration to three issues.
The first concerned 'a campaign aimed at restoring the collapse of
the system of social values and addressing corruption in its broadest sense'; the second involved 'the compilation of a consolidated
report on the government's efforts to deal with corruption'; lastly he
was asked to consider, 'the nature of the campaign, the participants
and a framework for implementation'.[67] The moral overtones of
government's concern, their recognition of the systemic nature of
corruption in the country, and the political will to devise a counter-
active framework should not be overlooked. The primary benefit in
the broadest sense of the fight against corruption was to be the restora-
tion of the moral fabric of South African society.

Omar subsequently appointed a committee to make recommendations to him. This committee was to be headed by Dr Bernie
Fanaroff of the National Crime Prevention Strategy secretariat, representatives from SAPS, the National Intelligence Agency (NIA), and
the Ministry of Justice. By July 1998 the committee was able to produce through substantial work involving research and consultation
a report detailing a series of recommendations for Omar's consideration. These proposals were included in a Cabinet memorandum
that was approved on 23 September 1998 and constituted the first
set of policy guidelines for implementation in the fight against
corruption.[68] The significance of this step should not be ignored,
as for the first time in South Africa's history a government had by

implication accepted that corruption was a serious problem requiring practical measures for its control. The report itself was the first attempt by anyone anywhere to carefully study the measures necessary to combat and prevent corruption in the South African public sector. Yet because it was written primarily to brief the Minister of Justice and his Cabinet colleagues on how to tackle corruption, the report was classified 'secret' and remains unpublished. The proposals adopted by Cabinet, however, were made public and these are worth mentioning.

Effective investigation and prosecution of corruption was considered paramount in the proposals and was to include breaches concerning payment of government taxes, state tendering, government purchases, disclosures by public officials, and insider trading within private companies. Mention was also made of the need for a feasibility study on the question of a single anti-corruption agency and the rationalization of existing agencies. The need for new legislation, a new strategy with due consideration to public service corruption, a statement of political intent from the president, a national summit, business co-operation, and greater levels of accountability from public officials were all listed for attention, in order to take the fight against corruption forward.

Understandably, the substantive response of government as contained in these measures was couched within the law enforcement framework, despite the recognition that 'investigation is in the long term unaffordable and unsustainable and is in any case much less cost-effective than prevention'.[69] It was also clearly established that the fight against corruption required political commitment that had to be matched by a willingness 'to commit the necessary resources'. This recognition of the costs of fighting corruption at the outset of policy deliberations is highly significant in view of concerns we have raised about how to fight corruption effectively.

Even where the establishment of a new anti-corruption agency was contemplated in the Cabinet proposals, it had to be 'properly resourced'. In terms of the initial report, Cabinet was urged to recognize that 'an effective fight against corruption will require enormous resources'.[70] Thus while the attention given to costs was included in the proposals, it seemed to have been a more critical consideration when the report was originally written. This very important factor in ensuring efficacy of implementation was unfortunately lost in the adaptation of the report into concrete proposals for action by the Department of Justice. Whether this was deliberately or unwittingly done is difficult to ascertain. The report called for a budget to be created which would lead to the establishment of an anti-corruption agency, but no funds were made available for this purpose in the short term. Thus, while national government was eager to flex its muscle of authority in firming up an agenda of actions against corruption, no serious consideration appears to have been given to the monetary implications of such actions. This might seem odd as most policy measures proposed within Cabinet are required to be submitted with due consideration given to their budgetary implications. But government could hardly have been at such a stage in its operations as to contemplate action of this sort if it faced other more pressing budgetary constraints and if corruption did not matter as much. Or, there might have been an unwritten consensus that the costs of fighting corruption would have to be largely borne out of the existing budgets of departments and agencies without the allocation of any new or special funds. Either way, the implementation of policy measures against corruption would be difficult to sustain without the necessary resources.

Turning the tide

To underscore the growing sense of urgency that 'a new proactive approach to combat corruption' was needed, and to promote its constitutional obligations of transparency, clean government and efficient service delivery, the Mandela administration initiated a public sector conference against corruption, which was held in parliament's Old Assembly Chamber in November 1998.[71] Apart from developing some concrete plans to combat and prevent corruption in the public sector, this conference was intended to provide a platform to prepare for the national summit and announce government's unequivocal support for the fight against corruption. The then Deputy President Mbeki in his keynote address spoke of a 'zero tolerance' approach whereby 'Government is firmly committed to coming down harshly on all forms of corruption including bribery and the abuse of public trust.'[72] New measures were to include new legislation, whistle-blower protection, bolstering the criminal justice system and a national campaign against corruption. Likewise, the Minister for the Public Service and Administration, Dr Zola Skweyiya, in his opening statement to the conference, emphasized that 'there must be zero tolerance for corrupt behaviour and practices'.

Justice Minister Omar reminded delegates in his speech that their struggle was against 'something that can threaten the whole edifice and social fabric of democracy, the rule of law, and the human rights culture' that was taking shape in the country. Corruption, together with crime, was now posing a serious threat to the stability and security of the country and had to be confronted.[73]

The historical significance of this event should not be underestimated. This was the first occasion in South Africa's history when the precincts of parliament were opened for discussion, involving most components of the public sector, on such a sensitive subject as corruption. Fortunately, most of the time was not taken up lamenting the corrupting legacy of the past, but in devising new strategies for future action through group discussions. The final conference statement, which was subsequently adopted as a policy directive by Cabinet, gives a strong indication of the emerging consensus of the time regarding public sector reform for the control of corruption. It proclaimed the struggle to end corruption to be the same struggle as that to transform government and society as a whole, and committed public officials to developing a strategy that combined 'prevention with ruthless action against aggressions'.[74] An 'ethos of public service, discipline and accountability' was called for where managers would declare their private assets in a register, sign performance agreements, enforce the Code of Conduct for the Public Service, and ensure better financial management and control to prevent corruption, and where government undertook to 'improve the capacity and efficiency of investigation and prosecution of corruption'.[75] Delegates further agreed that the private sector should form part of the 'solution' in reforming public sector procurement, with banks and auditors playing a more critical role in combating corruption. A working committee representing the stakeholders from among those present was tasked with taking forward the implementation process of the measures adopted and preparing for the forthcoming summit on corruption.

Public applause

Most sections of the media reported extensively on the public sector conference, with the deputy president's speech often being reprinted in mass-circulation newspapers.[76] The Mandela government, it seemed, had put the nation – including many opposition (political) parties – at ease, in stating its case against corruption unreservedly.

The political intent to act decisively against corrupt individuals, as stated at the conference, was a welcome sign of relief for many who doubted the ruling party's ability to clamp down on its own guilty members. In addition to the issues mentioned above, case studies were offered on good practice in fighting corruption, with inputs from the Department of Home Affairs, the South African Revenue Service, parliament, the Post Office, Mpumalanga and KwaZulu-Natal provinces, SAPS and the Department of Welfare. Group discussions were also held to cover the reform agenda for local government, strategic co-ordination of anti-corruption agencies, discipline, the criminal justice system, procurement and financial management. The public sector had for the first time gathered to collectively consider the problem of corruption, and succeeded in getting its constituent parts to commit to a common struggle against the effects of corruption on the country as a whole. This was significant, as it provided a basis for government to consider holding a broader cross-sectoral event to develop a national strategy against corruption.

Collective vision

Unfortunately, again, as alluded to in government's earlier attempts, no mention was made anywhere or at any time during the two-day proceedings of the budgetary implications of the measures put forward to fight corruption. Nor was the need for a cost-benefit analysis acknowledged, as the public sector representatives seemed quite oblivious of the monetary implications of their noble aspirations. The conference itself, as an event in the unfolding programme of government actions against corruption, was almost fully supported with funds from the UK's Department for International Development. The conventional understanding was that the country had sufficient resources to adapt to changing demands that arose from time to time and so the matter of resources was considered secondary. Government, it seemed, had pledged to henceforth plunge itself into a 'zero tolerance' mode of tackling corruption, with no thought given to the budgetary resources required for such an approach to succeed. It was also unclear following the conference as to who exactly was to do what to ensure that political will found expression in policy. The chairperson of the Public Service Commission, Stan Sangweni, would henceforth initiate a series of meetings with various stakeholders to prepare the country for the national summit on corruption. But he was powerless to ensure that resolutions passed in Cape

Town would be implemented in all public sector entities and state departments. The risk of failure, of this public sector initiative on corruption being viewed as serving the mere purpose of political prattling, was one that government therefore had to guard against.

It is clear that South Africa had barely started walking the road of democracy after its repressive past when alarm bells of concern for the moral fibre of the nation began to sound. Religious leaders, we should note, took pride of place in pointing to what they termed 'a deep moral crisis' that had engulfed the country by 1998.[77] They began a process of engaging the political leadership in a series of moral summits to evaluate reasons for the moral impasse and chart the way towards the renewal of society. Crime levels had ascended to about the highest in the world, with instances of rape, murder, robbery, car hijacking, child molestation, domestic violence and corruption spiralling out of control. Through the National Religious Leaders' Forum, a 'Code of Conduct for persons in positions of responsibility' was developed so that South Africans could 'live honest and upright lives and provide a heritage of love and prosperity for future generations'.[78] These calls did not go unheard, as President Mandela was the first to sign this code when he launched it, and he himself, in opening parliament in early 1999, decried those cadres in various government departments 'who are as corrupt as – if not more than – those they found in government'.[79] The scourge of corruption was making South Africa a 'sick society' whose future depended on a resolution of this debilitating problem.

Almost in anticipation of such a disturbing situation, prominent cleric and anti-apartheid activist Dr Beyers Naudé had seized the moment to initiate the formation of the national chapter of Transparency International in South Africa as early as 1997.[80] This followed from a seminar held jointly by TI and the Africa Leadership Forum in 1995 in Pretoria, at which Naudé pleaded for civil society to 'take hands and act in unison' in forging a new coalition against corruption.[81] The extensive consultative process that preceded the national summit involved all sectors of South African society, with a view to obtaining critical information about all such activities that were directed against corruption. The private sector was no mere passive observer in this situation as the release of a corporate governance report, produced by the Johannesburg-based Institute of Directors under Judge Merwyn King, offered guidelines regarding responsibilities to shareholders, relations with customers and suppliers, employment practices, accounting practices, insider trading, social responsibility, and other such matters. The National Anti-Corruption Summit, after it took place in April 1999, would therefore serve as the most critical milestone in the country's short struggle against corruption. It was a struggle largely inspired by President Mandela, but which found expression among most of his Cabinet ministers, other senior officials in the public sector, community and religious leaders, and among the rank and file of South Africans of all races. A new president was to assume office soon after the summit, but a collective vision, tentative strategy and national consensus to combat corruption were already in place.

National summit

The national summit was again held in the precincts of parliament, with funding secured from the European Union for its organization. Unlike the earlier effort, government now sought to 'develop a clearly articulated national strategy to fight corruption in all sectors of society', to obtain a commitment thereto, and to recommend legislative measures where necessary.[82] The delegates, drawn from all sectors of South African life (but significantly excluding representatives of parliamentary opposition parties), were unanimous that corruption adversely affected all, but especially the poor, was corroding the national culture and ethos of democracy, was furthermore a blight on society caused by the worship of self, and required a 'culture of zero tolerance' to bring it under control. The resolutions adopted drew attention to a plethora of issues, including the need for legislative review, whistle-blowing mechanisms, support for open democracy, special courts, 'blacklisting', a national co-ordinating structure, hotlines, disciplinary action, ethics, codes of conduct, education and training, research and analysis, and the need for a sustained media campaign. Cabinet was of course only too willing to adopt this agenda as a good governance policy imperative by July 1999, particularly as it resonated strongly with measures it had been contemplating since 1997.

Despite the presence at the summit of participants from civil society, organized labour and the private sector, commitments were again made to the nation without due consideration of their potential impact on the national budget or the cost of effectively implementing such measures. The law enforcement approach to fighting corruption again took precedence, but amid a range of other tasks for most sections of society. A partnership of shared interests was now possible as government, business and civil society pledged their resolve to fight a common enemy jointly. Some business leaders were inspired to the extent of producing an ethics code for business practices, but this was subsequently not adopted by any national or local formation.

Civil society might have enjoyed a greater measure of success as it moved to organize the first national civil society conference on corruption. This eventually took place in August 2000 after a lengthy participatory process involving workshops held in the provinces.[83] The mechanism that was meant to take the national initiative forward, however, in terms of a summit resolution was the 'National Co-ordinating Structure with the authority to effectively lead, co-ordinate, monitor and manage the National Anti-Corruption Programme'. This was clearly the most onerous task identified by the summit, that is, the creation of a super cross-sectoral structure that would lead and manage the national fight against corruption. It would unfortunately take a full two years before any kind of progress on this particular matter could be reported.

A forum without substance

In terms of the United Nations Global Programme against Corruption (GPAC), once a country has formulated its anti-corruption strategy, a national integrity steering committee or its equivalent should be formed as 'the watchdog and mechanism to launch, implement and monitor a country's national integrity strategy'.[84] In Hong Kong, as we saw earlier (see pp. 58–61), community involvement was regarded as paramount for successful implementation of the anti-corruption strategy. Advisory cross-sectoral committees were appointed to closely monitor the work of the Independent Commission Against Corruption, and were encouraged to 'regularly brief the media on their work, including any advice they may have given to the Commissioner on major issues'.[85] Against the background of South Africa's transition to a participatory democracy, it was not unexpected that the national summit would recommend a cross-sectoral approach to monitoring the implementation of the anti-corruption strategy. Thereafter, the Public Service Commission was mandated by government to establish a cross-sectoral task team to consider proposals that would lead to the eventual creation of an anti-corruption entity, as had been decided at the summit. This process began in August 1999 with representatives from state departments, parliament, constitutional oversight bodies, parastatals (large state-owned corporations formed for commercial purposes), civil society, business and organized labour meeting regularly in Pretoria. The final text of a draft constitution for the new agency, however, was found to be problematic, as the thought of an independent body taking on functions normally resident with the executive arm of government was rejected. It was accepted instead that government had ultimate responsibility to formulate and implement policy, particularly with regard to combating corruption. A compromise was reached, which involved setting up a non-statutory advisory body comprising equal representation (ten members each) from business, civil society and government. Its purpose was to contribute to 'a national consensus through co-ordination of sectoral strategies against corruption', advise government, and share information on best practice in fighting corruption. The National Anti-Corruption Forum was consequently formed on the basis of these vague principles and formally launched by Deputy President Jacob Zuma in Langa, Cape Town, on 15 June 2001.[86]

The first full meeting of the NACF took place a month after its launch, with most sectoral representatives, including Cabinet ministers, in attendance. Subsequent attempts to convene meetings or deliver on the purposes for which the forum was established failed dismally, however. It seemed that while the public sector, with government as the lead agent, was pressing ahead in implementing the resolutions of the summit, the private sector lagged behind. This was to be expected to some extent because while the summit resolutions were adopted as part of government's strategy, business in general showed little concern. A fairly low-key level of representation was delegated to participate in the forum despite the high level of public sector members designated by government. It is possible to infer that when the notion of a national agency to fight corruption was conceived at the summit, it was done in haste and in confusion with the view that the country needed a strong, central agency with legal authority to lead the struggle against corruption. How an institution comprising all sectors of society, but without legal authority, could serve a useful purpose is uncertain. A structure allowing for full democratic participation by all stakeholders who would work together in 'partnership' against corruption seemed so full of potential, yet was so weak in operation.

Civil society remained a highly fragmented entity when the forum was formed, and it was always unclear as to who the legitimate representatives of this sector were. A prominent attorney of the National Democratic Lawyers Association who had played a leading role in the forum's formation, Adv Dali Mpofu, was put forward by other civil society members to be the first chairperson. Government seemed happy to accept this proposal, provided that the chairmanship was decided on a rotational basis among the sectors. Civil society, and its first chairperson, regrettably failed to execute any functions of the forum, much to the consternation of the National Religious Leaders' Forum, who raised the matter with President Mbeki early in 2002. The Minister for the Public Service and Administration, Geraldine Fraser-Moleketi, was requested by the president forthwith to take the lead in the 'revitalization' of the forum as 'a matter of urgency'. Despite her enthusiastic attempts to call meetings of the forum periodically, the interest shown towards this initiative by all sectors remained very poor. Government-designated ministers usually absented themselves from meetings because of other engagements, civil society members were never at ease in representing the interests of so diverse a constituency, and business representatives were themselves divided by a multiplicity of formations within their ranks.

To expect the forum to articulate a national consensus around issues of corruption with one voice under these conditions was therefore somewhat preposterous and naïve. No executive committee meetings were held because there was no finality as to the composition of such a committee. Yet none of the above reasons for the forum's failure are as compelling as the fact that it was an institution established without a budget. The memorandum of understanding that brought the forum into being indicated that it was to be 'assisted by a secretariat provided by the Public Service Commission'. This involved staff in the commission's office in Pretoria spending much of their time trying to synchronize the diaries of very busy individuals to attend occasional meetings and little else. Such meetings, if they involved lengthy inputs from government, as was usual, were held in venues hired and sponsored by donors. It is quite clear that the forum had no hope of functioning effectively without the required resources. It is almost inconceivable that a country would attempt to create a national structure with the expressed purpose of containing something like a contagious disease without the requisite funds being made available. Worse still, this was a matter that was only given attention in February 2004 when a foreign donor roundtable was convened by Minister Fraser-Moleketi. As late as July 2004, more than three years after its formation, the NACF secretariat received a directive to compile a budgetary request for the consideration of the National Treasury. While the customary fiscal approach on the part of government in the fight against corruption, namely engaging the support of donor agencies while leaving the coffers of the National Treasury relatively untouched, was still being followed, signs of a shift were slowly beginning to emerge.

Cost of commitment

South Africa's transition to democracy under the leadership of Nelson Mandela brought an end to hundreds of years of racial segregation and created the basis for a new society to be built on the ruins of apartheid. This new society, unfortunately, was not one free of corruption. If apartheid was a form of institutionalized corruption, especially in the 'homelands', many of its essential features were not obliterated overnight, but carried over into the new political dispensation. Yet with the rise of organized crime and South Africa's readmission into the international community, corruption began to assume a new and peculiar character that required state intervention. This began in 1997 when Cabinet commissioned its groundbreaking study that identified, among other concerns, the need for substantial resources to make the fight against corruption effective. While the public sector approach received fresh impetus from a historic conference held in parliament in 1998, it was only at the national summit held the following year that a national strategy was articulated. This was achieved in close consultation with representatives of labour, business, the faith communities, and civil society who with government would later form the National Anti-Corruption Forum. While this body has remained largely ineffective, its creation was symbolic of a national consensus that was emerging on the urgent need to combat and prevent corruption. The time previously spent in deliberations about how to fight corruption was now to be taken up by implementation of the national strategy against it.

Unfortunately, despite the adoption of a national strategy to fight corruption, it was far from clear how, when and where funding would be secured to ensure implementation. Such a question had not been posed when the strategy was being adopted, even though the issue of resources had been emphasized in a critical study commissioned by Cabinet. Policy shifts in fighting corruption were clearly agreed upon in the absence of policy analysis, which in this instance should have included the calculation of costs and benefits. As we saw earlier, policymaking in South Africa since 1994 had shown a penchant toward achieving 'mixed success and ambivalence', of paying only 'lip service' and confusing 'policy advocacy with policy analysis', and of 'governing by legislation rather than sound administration'. The nation was now being taken into the corruption battlefields with the threat that such policy contradictions would be repeated. From the holding of the first public sector conference on corruption to the formation of the NACF, no funds from the National Treasury were committed for the unfolding of the national strategy. This must rank as a catastrophic failure of the Mandela government in its fight against corruption, which, as we have seen, was remarkable for its creation of a national strategy and commitment to the moral transformation of society.

6

Bribery and the Bible

Mixed messages

Our understanding of why corruption might be a curse to the world today is unfortunately not helped by the double message or ambivalence about the problem in the Christian scriptures. Some will attempt to claim biblical authority to bolster the fight against corruption but, as we shall see, such authority is difficult to prove on the basis of textual evidence alone. This of course does not imply that if we accept such ambiguity, it then provides us with a moral defence for engaging in corrupt practices. It might be argued, as I hope to show, that the evidence of scripture is theologically 'sufficient' to enable the development from a Christian moral point of view of an unequivocal condemnation of corruption in most of its manifestations. It cannot be assumed, on the other hand, that the Bible provides us with moral laws which can be used as concrete prescriptions to solve problems that were unimaginable thousands of years ago.[1] While bribery as an 'unclean' exchange is something as ancient as creation itself, corruption understood as the misuse of public power for private benefit is very much a twentieth-century phenomenon. Unless one chooses to read the Bible backwards, projecting an alien context into its canonical history to decipher its teachings, we may find that using scriptural verses to justify human behaviour today is quite misleading. There is still a fundamental human value that the Bible, if taken as God's Word, bears witness to, namely, that corruption is an anathema in our time that must be expunged from society.

The Old Testament

Genesis might be a logical starting point for us to unravel the many instances of 'exchange' in word and deed that offered the possibility of a bribe being either accepted or rejected. We read of the serpent pointing out to Eve the possible benefits she would gain by eating the apple (Gen. 3.1–7). But as the serpent does not make her an 'offer' this gesture cannot be construed as a bribe. Eve is condemned because her sin was one of disobedience, and there is no hint of her having been 'bought off' to behave in the way she did. Delilah was similarly tempted when the Philistines offered her 1,100 pieces of silver to share with them the secret of Samson's strength (Judges 16.4–22). Yet this action is not equated in any way with an offer of a *bribe* as the focus in the story is on Delilah's betrayal of her husband and his complete trust in her. Unlike some sexual sins in Genesis where the punishment is deserving of death, we struggle to find instances of law enforcement or biblical sanction against bribery. 1 Samuel provides a case in point because of its 'mixed message' where Saul sentences his son Jonathan to death for his disobedience. His people seek to save him so they 'ransom Jonathan' by paying Saul, who takes the ransom but does not incur any penalty for the 'sin' of accepting it (1 Sam. 14.45). While Saul is portrayed as sinful, Samuel is himself the noble judge who can do no wrong, and even when he is guilty of boasting idly, he is allowed restitution (1 Sam. 12.3). Thus Samuel is described as a good judge whose sons, Joel and Abiah, 'take gifts [*shohadh*] and pervert justice' (1 Sam. 8.3) without condemnation from their father.

There are, however, other examples in scripture where condemnation of bribery is unequivocal. Take Deuteronomy where, among the instructions given to judges, they are explicitly told: 'Do not accept a bribe, for a bribe blinds the eyes of the wise and twists the words . . .' (Deut. 17.1). A bribe is thus viewed quite negatively, something associated with the wicked who 'take a bribe from the bosom to stretch the way of justice' (Prov. 17.23). The standard term used to denote an act of offering or receiving a bribe is *shohadh*, the same term used to describe a gift. The term is therefore neutral and is also used to point to an expected and fitting tribute to a superior person. Gift giving is mentioned right at the outset of Genesis where Cain is found bringing the produce of the soil as 'a gift to the LORD' and Abel likewise brings the fat portions of his new flock to the Lord (Gen. 4.3–4). Israel as a nation is warned by God not to 'come into my presence empty-handed' (Exod. 23.15, 34.20) but with gifts. The community is called to a festival gathering three times a year but no one is to come without gifts (Deut. 16.16). Yet as the story of Cain and Abel shows, God will only accept the gift of a worthy giver. This is later made clear in Proverbs: 'The wicked man's sacrifice is abominable to the LORD' (15.8). When the upright Noah is rewarded, it is because he has made sacrifices and brought gifts to God (Gen. 9.9). God's response is to initiate the covenant with Noah on the back of such reciprocity.

In Amos, the rulers who turn 'justice itself into poison' have their gifts rejected for they are told by God: 'When you present your sacrifices and offerings I will not accept them' (Amos 5.23). In Isaiah (1.23), judges who 'are greedy for offerings and itch for presents' are denounced as the 'offer of your gifts is useless' (1.11–13). Elsewhere, Isaiah makes clear that 'The man who lives an upright life and speaks the truth, who scorns to enrich himself with loot, who snaps his fingers at offering, that is the man who shall dwell on the heights' (Isa. 33.15–16). This exhortation might be a later version of the saying in Psalm 15, where the man who does what is right is identified as the one who 'takes no *shohadh* concerning an innocent man'. The wicked man, however, is he who in Proverbs 'accepts *shohadh* under his cloak to pervert the course of justice' (17.13), while 'he who spurns gifts and presents [*mattana*] will enjoy long life' (17.23).

There are seemingly instances in Proverbs where bribery or corrupt behaviour is condoned. We read for example that 'A gift widens the way for people; it leads them to important people' (18.16). One can argue that this verse should not be understood in a sarcastic way but with due recognition to 'the circumstance of the gift'. If it is given with the purpose of circumventing justice, then it must be wrong.[2] But given in situations with good intentions, it can lead to the opening of doors for good ends. We also read that 'A gift in secret calms anger; and a hidden bribe passionate wrath' (21.14). One way around this apparent contradiction is to assume that in Proverbs the speakers merely 'observe and describe (rather than advocate) what they know to be a reality in human communities', that they do not consider all bribes equal, and that when judiciously given, bribes can create new opportunities and 'defuse potentially dangerous situations'.[3] This would require that we understand these sayings in Proverbs to have been given 'tongue in cheek', but such a view seems unwarranted at best. Weighed together with the overall lack of sanctions against the practice of bribery, it might be more plausible to assume that the Old Testament as a whole, including Proverbs, reflects the state of affairs in a permissive and tolerant society.

The New Testament

When we turn to the New Testament, we find only one direct reference to the expectation of a bribe. This involves Felix, the Roman governor of Judea, and Paul: 'At the same time he hoped that money would be given him by Paul. So sending for him often, Felix conversed with him' (Acts 24.26). Had Paul given Felix money, he might have been freed, but such bribery would have been illegal, even if such a law was often ignored. Instead, Paul is kept in prison and out of harm's way as a favour to the Jewish leadership. The context of this encounter is related to Felix's interest in the Way of the gospel and the expectation of a bribe is not strange if we accept that people can have mixed motives. Less direct is Simon's offer to Peter to have the authority to distribute the Spirit by offering to pay for it (Acts 8.19). Peter's rebuke of Simon amounts to a forthright condemnation of the one giving a bribe, something that was clearly absent in the Old Testament where retribution was usually directed to the bribe takers, if at all. In both of the above cases, the act of bribery is alluded to but not consummated in any way, so further judgment is suspended.

One incident involving an exchange of information stands out as an act of corruption by our definition, though it is not viewed as such in the New Testament. After the resurrection, the chief priests ask the Roman soldiers to report that the body of Jesus has been stolen by his disciples. In return they receive a large sum of money and their false report is apparently widely circulated (Matt. 28.11–15). In their time, these soldiers might have accepted the money as gifts or presents and probably saw little harm in false reporting over an isolated occurrence.

The Gospel writers also take a very dim view of some sales of goods, suggesting a moral judgment on their part. The first involves those 'who sold doves' in the Temple (Mark 11.15–16) and were driven out by Jesus,[4] while the second is the sale of Jesus himself. Judas goes to the high priests and offers to betray Jesus, for which he is promised a sum of money (Mark 26.14–16). Yet in none of these isolated reciprocities is a biblical precept being espoused; rather, we seem to be shown cases when human transactions have gone wrong because of ulterior motives. On the other hand, in Luke's Gospel, the biblical message about the consequences of corrupt behaviour is much more clearly articulated and deserving of careful scrutiny.

Giving and receiving in Luke

If Mediterranean society provides the backdrop and social location for much of the New Testament writings, including Luke, understanding its social institutions becomes important for the interpretation of texts. For our purposes, we are particularly interested in the basic but pervasive form of dependency relations at the time of Jesus involving the reciprocal exchange of goods and services between patrons (usually strong and superior) and their clients (socially inferior and weak). These power relations were the pillars of both public and private life, but have often been ignored by modern scholars who tend to 'assume for the ancient world political and social structures akin to their own, [and] have failed to note, or have dismissed as insignificant, the prevalence and meaning of a pattern of social relations so alien to their own social experience and democratic values'.[5] Such a judgment might appear harsh, but it would explain why we know so little about the prevalence of corruption in New Testament times despite its being a feature of everyday life. Patrons and clients inhabited a world then (as they do now!) that was quintessentially defined by unequal power relations, influence, power brokers, benefactors, pay-offs and trade-offs, networks, contacts in high places, right connections, honour and prestige, loyalty and commitment, favours and of course, money.

The patronage system that prevailed in Palestine at the time of Jesus was one inherited from the Romans but which had 'degenerated into petty favour seeking and manipulation' and where '[c]lients competed for patrons just as patrons competed for clients in an often desperate struggle to gain economic or political advantage.'[6] Powerful patrons were those with access to vast resources like water, food, jobs, land and money and who used their influence to hand out favours based on friendships, favouritism and personal knowledge. Clients were at the mercy of such patrons, to whom they owed loyalty, public recognition and honour. To survive, clients needed to be dependent on their superiors, but in a chaotic situation it was not uncommon for them to switch allegiance from one form of dependency to another. Between these two players were the brokers, those who relied on the generosity of the patrons to act as mediators in helping them dispose of their goods and services. They might be city officials or religious leaders, or even prophets. They offered a strategic contact point between both patron and client and worked the system so as to increase their power base. Clients might boast of being friends with their patrons, but friendship was normally reserved for social equals. These bonds of reciprocity should not be overlooked when we try to understand why human beings coalesced under the burden of 'obligation' and behaved in ways we might now judge as corrupt.

Luke mentions a common case of the 'patronage hierarchy' at work involving all of these players in a single episode, one that included Jesus himself.

> Now a centurion had a slave who was dear to him; he was sick and at the point of death. When he heard of Jesus, he sent to him elders of the Jews asking him to come and heal his slave. And when they came to Jesus, they besought him earnestly, saying, 'He is worthy to have you do this to him, for he loves our nation, and he built us our synagogue.' And Jesus went with them, and when he was not far from the house, the centurion sent friends to say to him, 'Lord, do not trouble yourself, for I am not worthy to have you come under my roof; therefore I did not presume to come to you. But only speak the word, and let my servant be healed. For I also am a man set under authority, with soldiers under me; and I say to one, "Go," and he goes, and to another, "Come," and he comes, and to my slave, "Do this," and the slave does it.' When Jesus heard this he was amazed at him, and turning to the crowd that followed him, he said, 'I tell you, not even in Israel have I found such faith.' When those who had been sent returned to the house, they found the slave in good health.
>
> (Luke 7.1–10)

The centurion in this account is clearly the power broker with resources at his disposal for the citizenry, and we are informed that he has performed the task of distribution well. He sends the elders to Jesus hoping that they can mediate for him with what Jesus can offer. Despite his authority to instruct clients, he sends 'friends' to tell Jesus that he does not regard him as such but as a superior instead. This impresses Jesus, for here is a centurion placing faith in him, as God's broker, and he delivers the healing as requested. This implies a reversal of roles as the centurion becomes the client at God's mercy.

Some understand the language of grace as used by Jesus to reflect the social reality of the patronage system, where God is the 'Ultimate Patron' who graciously distributes his 'wares' through the mediation of Jesus.[7] Others go further to show that the concept is rooted in the everyday experiences of peasant society and the relations between the 'haves' and the 'have nots'.[8] For Luke it is clear that one cannot be a client of both God and the system of greed (Luke 16.13). The main characteristics of the patron–client relationship are not diluted by their transposition to the divine realm. These include the offer of support and protection which a client receives, and which is reciprocated with expressions of loyalty, solidarity and goodwill; high levels of commitment in relations, bringing personal honour and a series of obligations; the possibility that such relations may be entered into on a voluntary basis and may endure over time; and the norm whereby such relations are defined by differences in status and power. The hierarchy of patronage would extend throughout all levels of society and the task of 'making friends' was thus a challenge for everyone (Luke 7.6), and those with only a few friends would suffer social embarrassment. Not surprisingly, Jesus was viewed as a 'friend' of sinners then, just as much as when we use such language today in singing of him bearing our sins. Similarly, when we offer prayer, praise and honour to God, it's in the same vein as the performance of rituals required of clients who regularly brought honour to and enhanced the reputation of their superiors by their public gestures towards them.

In Luke's Gospel only, we read of a parable told by Jesus about an 'unrighteous judge' who feared neither God nor any human being. For our purposes, the context, meaning and point of this parable is secondary to the probability that we are presented here with an image of God as a corrupt judge!

> [Jesus] said, 'In a certain city there was a judge who neither feared God nor had respect for people. In that city there was a widow who kept on coming to him and saying, "Grant me justice against my opponent." For a while he refused; but later he said to himself, "Though I have no fear of God and no respect for anyone, yet because this widow keeps bothering me, I will grant her justice, so that she may not wear me out by continually coming."' And the Lord said, 'Listen to what the unjust judge says'. (Luke 18.2–6)

We need to recognize that the judge in this parable is shameless, with no care in the world as to how others might perceive his actions, and contrasted with him is one of the most vulnerable persons of society, a widow. Women did not ordinarily appear in courtrooms, so we must assume that this woman had no male family member to represent her. Lest he suffer public disgrace, the judge eventually agrees to take up her case. Bribery would appear to form the background to this case, for here is the poorest of the poor, unable to pay and being refused justice until she can come up with a 'brown envelope' to facilitate the resolution of her case. For no other reason is the judge slow to act.[9] The analogy of God as an unrighteous judge, let alone a corrupt one, is somewhat troubling to us for it seems to suggest that disgraceful behaviour may have an air of respectability or be tacitly tolerated. God is nowhere in scripture likened to an adulterer or incestuous man, as no greater repugnance was possible than that towards sexual sins. But if 'corruption' assumed its peculiar forms through the patronage system and had infiltrated society at all levels, it might well have shown the face of a lesser evil. This was something known to everyone, part and parcel of daily life, and hence worthy of analogy even to the personhood of God, by none other than Jesus, without the fear of wrath from any quarter.

Reversal of misfortune in Luke-Acts

By mentioning the parable of the unjust judge in his Gospel, Luke should not summarily be dismissed as a supporter of the status quo as far as the culture of patronage was concerned. On the contrary, he has a clearly defined agenda to show how Jesus overthrows the power of those at the top and reorders the terms and conditions of reciprocity or exchange. In peasant society, it was possible to base human transactions of life on different forms of exchange.[10] There was a 'generalized' form of reciprocity, where the altruistic motive dominated often in an extreme form, with the 'pure gift' the ideal. 'Balanced' reciprocity created a situation where interests (of both patron and clients) were amicably served, with disruptions possible if a gift was given and not reciprocated. 'Negative' reciprocity was the 'unsocial extreme' where one party would seek to 'get something for nothing' in violent or other ways. Jesus enters the house of a leader of the Pharisees to have a meal and tells him this parable:

> When you give a luncheon or a dinner, do not invite your friends or your brothers or your relatives or rich neighbours, in case they may invite you in return, and you would be repaid. But when you give a banquet, invite the poor, the crippled, the lame, and the blind. And you will be blessed because they cannot repay you, for you will be repaid at the resurrection of the righteous. (Luke 14.12–14)

The guest lists in this parable differ according to the social location of the invitees, but also in 'their capacity to reciprocate'.[11] In the first list, the reciprocity is balanced between equals within a close circle of friends. These are people close to one another, of similar rank and status, with corresponding levels of wealth. Hospitality in their context operates on a selfish principle of being invited in return, as by such means group identity is sustained and social bonds strengthened. Jesus now challenges the Pharisees to break out of this myopic view of the world by urging them to extend their hospitality to outsiders – the poor, crippled, the lame and the blind. This is more than a test for community cohesion; it puts religion on the line as these outsiders are considered ritually unclean. The point made by Jesus is that the Pharisees should opt instead for a system of exchange where reciprocity does not matter, at least in this life. The rich and powerful should 'disinterestedly' invite the lowly to their table fellowships in sure knowledge that there will be no repayment from those who have not the necessary means at their disposal to reciprocate. The temptation to behave corruptly is immediately dissipated, as the outsiders have nothing to 'offer' their rich hosts and are in this context 'beyond' influence in any way.

It should be clear that Jesus is not announcing a general prohibition against spending time with one's friends and relatives. When he relates the parables of the lost sheep and the lost coin (Luke 15.3–7, 8–10), friends and neighbours are invited to celebrate the recovery of lost property. Elsewhere, Jesus again dilutes traditional exchange patterns relating to the lending of money when he urges, 'And if you lend to those from whom you hope to receive, of what credit is that to you? Even sinners lend to sinners, to receive as much again' (6.34). Again, the balanced reciprocity that was generally practised is overturned with an exhortation to lend while 'expecting nothing in return' (6.35). This can only be understood in a most revolutionary sense, for it marks the 'end of the patron-client relationship in the traditional sense'.[12] These relationships were premised on inequality and the exchange of different resources – patrons owned the economic means of production while their clients, who used such means, requited with salutes, honour, loyalty and solidarity. The power dynamic changes if the generosity of the patron cannot be used for personal interest, that is, to further bolster the advantage the patron already has over the client. In the new form of reciprocity being introduced by Jesus, God becomes the Ultimate Patron who confers rewards in the hereafter. The notion of exchange is yet upheld, but payment for goods or services rendered is deferred or removed from the social equation of power.

On moving from the conflictual terrain of early Palestinian society to the early beginnings of the Christian Church, as recounted in Acts, Luke's 'moral economy' which Jesus had initiated is now put to work. No longer encumbered with the burdens of class struggle or status anxiety, Christians are set free to share all things in common. Individual ownership of property is now set aside as all things are shared.

> For no one among them was a needy person, for as many as were possessors of land or houses sold them, and were bringing the proceeds of what was sold and were setting them at the apostles' feet, and it was being distributed to each as one had need. (Acts 4.34–35)

This reflects the new standard for life in Christ: all members are family and friends to one another, a way of being achieved by the complete collapse of patronage reciprocity. Now all possible objects of exchange are disposed of towards a common purse, such as Jesus himself had kept among his disciples. Those who were elites before act in the interests of the poor now and the barriers of inequality come tumbling down. Barnabas is mentioned by name as one who sold his field. This reversal of the system of exchange is first experienced on the Day of Pentecost when everything is held in common, assets are disposed of and the proceeds distributed according to need, such that a situation of equality now prevails (Acts 2.44–45). The world that allowed differences in class and status to be exploited for economic advantage is abandoned by the first Christians in favour of one where reciprocity is based solely on need. Lest it be forgotten that this was taking place in the real world, Luke adds an episode involving Ananias and Sapphira, his wife, who are both struck dead for complicity in withholding part of the proceeds from the sale of property (Acts 5.1–11). Reciprocity is now based on one's relationship with the Ultimate Benefactor as a form of 'horizontal solidarity' takes root which might have served to prevent 'primitive Christian communities from becoming the social clientele for some rich patron'.[13] The previously aggressive diatribes against the rich are absent in Acts as the community of the faithful is reconstituted as one in the absent world of rich and poor, patron and clients, or for that matter saints and sinners.

Children of Abraham

The apparent ambiguity or mixed message about bribery that would seem to colour parts of the Old Testament, as we saw earlier, is also clarified in the teachings of Judaism. Jewish sources for scriptural authority include the Torah (the first five books of the Hebrew scriptures, Genesis to Deuteronomy), the Talmud (a collection of ancient rabbinic writings) and the Midrash (commentaries on the Hebrew scriptures). One of the normative principles of Jewish life that deserves particular mention and which the Hebrew scriptures constantly point towards is *tzedakah*, which requires a striving for social justice and engagement in righteous acts throughout one's life. Honesty and transparency are mandated in all business transactions, as the Holiness Code of Leviticus makes clear: 'You shall not steal, nor deal falsely, nor lie to one another' (19.11); 'You shall not defraud your neighbour or rob him' (19.13a). Writing in the *Jewish Ethicist*, Rabbi Asher Meir of the Business Ethics Centre of Jerusalem asserts:[14]

> Judaism's view of bribery is clear: 'Don't accept bribes, for bribery blinds even the wise and distorts even the words of the righteous' (Exod. 23.8). Although the verse refers to a judge, the rationale applies to anyone in a position of public trust. A person may rationalize accepting a bribe and convince himself that his judgement will be unaffected, but the Torah tells us that even a wise and righteous person can't avoid having his point of view influenced by a bribe.

Meir goes further and denounces payment of bribes to influence the behaviour of public officials. Stealing from the public coffers is the worst form of theft as, unlike in the case of an individual, you do not know who you stole from and cannot appease the person wronged. In deciding the outcome of legal disputes or distributing resources for the community, honesty and transparency are not alone mandatory, so also is the empowerment of the weak or those outside the power structure. Ruth Messinger of the American Jewish World Service finds evidence for this moral injunction in an example from the Torah: '[w]hen Jethro, a Medianite priest, visits his son-in-law Moses, he observes how Moses serves as a single judge for the whole Israelite population. Jethro instructs Moses to change this inefficient and burdensome practice by empowering the people to judge themselves, only in the hardest cases should their issues be brought before Moses (Exodus 18).'[15] This leads her to conclude that in Jewish ethics, making decisions in the public interest requires a framework of equity and fairness without deference to those one likes nor the spurning of those one dislikes.

Meir's advice is not necessarily found palatable, especially by those living in 'the real world and its discontents'. One anonymous respondent wrote back as follows:[16]

> Rabbi Asher's interpretation may be correct but the real world is rife with situations where bribery is the only rational course for a business person to take. As construction executives we constantly get hit up in the middle of a project for 'extras' from the police so that our deliveries, made in scrupulously legal fashion, receive the same traffic protection that our competitors have. Don't want to pay? Then you don't want any materials delivered to your jobsite for a few weeks. Since you're already half done, they know they got you over a barrel. You have a contract to fulfil and they've got a need for 'extras'. It gets worse when their superiors get involved. They want more than the beat cops. If you stubbornly refuse to pay, they may start destroying your equipment. A few well placed 9 mm bullets can hash up an engine pretty effectively. Can you afford to put a lot of your valuable employees out of work, lose a good chunk of your hard-earned capital, ruin your future credit rating, and spend countless fruitless hours trying to prosecute the police (a hysterically funny idea in many communities) over a few hundred dollars? So how many people's lives and fortunes are you going to ruin for your ideals? This is not an idle calculation, Rabbi, but an everyday dilemma for many hardworking people.

The other child in the Abrahamic household of faith is Islam, where the sovereignty of God is the highest principle governing all human conduct. The Islamic perspective on bribery is based on the (*sharia*) laws given by God (Allah) to the Holy Prophet in the Qur'an, where those who pay or receive bribes are cursed. The general principle to be followed in all business transactions enunciated in the Qur'an is one of justice: 'Deal not unjustly, and you shall not be dealt with unjustly' (2.279). Again, fair play and righteous conduct remains the norm: 'Woe to those that deal in fraud, – those who, when they have to receive by measure from men, exact full measure. But when they have to give by measure or weight to men, give less than due. Do they not think that they will be called to account?' (83.1–4).

In a book published by the International Institute of Islamic Thought (based in the United States), the principle of unity related to the Oneness of God to guide Islamic ethics is introduced. It requires that Muslims refrain from any form of discrimination among employees, suppliers or buyers on any other stakeholder on the basis of race, colour, sex or religion.[17] Support for this view is even found in the Qur'an: 'O mankind! Lo! We have created you male and female, and have made you nations and tribes, that you may know one another' (49.13). When matters arise which are of a nature not covered by Qur'anic revelation, Islamic scholars and legal experts are permitted to offer their opinions, which can be converted into regulations for human conduct. Bribery (*rashwah*) is generally condemned but there are apparently some cases where it is 'permissible' to pay a bribe if someone cannot have his or her rights attained in any other way. This is considered '*haraam*' (sinful) for the one who receives it, 'but it is not *haraam* for the one who gives it, because the giver is only giving it in order to get his rights, but the taker who takes the bribe is sinning because he has taken something that he does not deserve'.[18] The same judgment is expressed by another expert, as follows: 'But if a person has been deprived of his rights and he gives a bribe so as to ward off mistreatment from himself, this is permissible for the one who gives it but it is sin for the one who takes it.'[19] Some might argue that such an interpretation creates a window of opportunity for petty acts of bribery to be habitually condoned, when in fact the moral challenge is to overturn any systemic culture that offers a breeding ground for corrupt practices.

In an article put out by the Malaysian Institute of Islamic Understanding (IKIM), its deputy director, Sayed Othman Alhabshi, is adamant that Islam 'frowns upon' the 'sinful act' of bribery or corruption. He further notes that 'All benefits derived from sinful activities are definitely unlawful. To this applies the famous *hadith* [oral sayings of the Holy Prophet] which state that the flesh that grows out of unlawful income has no place in the hereafter but hell.'[20] For Alhabshi it is clear that 'if we bribe to get to a certain position, the stream of income that we enjoy from such a position is also questionable Islamically.'[21]

Thus, whether it is the tenets of Islam, Judaism or Christianity that are summoned to confront the ethics of corrupt behaviour, the consensus is clearly on the side of condemnation. On the part of Jesus Christ, the founder of Christianity, the rebuke might be framed in 'other-worldly' terms as he was more intent on establishing the 'upside-down Kingdom' of God where bribery or corruption would have had no place at all. As Albert Nolan remarks, this reign of God 'would thus not come down from above; it would rise up from below, from the poor, the little ones, the sinners, the outcasts, the lost, from the villages of Galilee. They would become like brothers and sisters who care for one another, identify with one another, protect one another and share with one another.'[22] Nepotism, one of the most common forms of corruption, would have no place in this world in view of the injunction given by Jesus: 'If anyone comes to me who does not hate his father, mother, wife, children, brothers, sisters, yes and his own life too, he cannot be my disciple' (Luke 14.26). There is no giving of preference if one is a member of God's family, and for this reason Jesus seems to shun his own family when they come looking for him (Mark 3.33). Nolan notes that 'Jesus wants to move beyond the limitations of the blood family of close relatives to the broader family of God's kingdom. An exclusive love for one's close family would be a form of group selfishness.'[23] We may say that bribery understood with a figurative meaning would be the attempt of people trying to buy their way into the Kingdom without the due diligence or exercise of non-preferential interest in the transactions of human life.

7

What can churches do?

Growing awareness

It will probably come as a shock to many readers to learn that there is an emerging body of literature which has, almost silently, pronounced a sweeping verdict on why some Christians are more prone to corruption than others, and why Muslims might be worse off than Christians in falling prey. The first point to be noted is that most of those succumbing to these hypotheses are working from an empirical and therefore scientific basis, which makes it difficult for their findings to be simplistically dismissed. However, a more serious concern relates to the absence of any theological underpinning to clarify their somewhat controversial results. Danish professor Martin Paldam was one of the first to postulate that Reformed Christians, among whom he included Protestants and Anglicans, were less corrupt than those belonging to the Orthodox and Catholic traditions.[1] For him, the Reformation was more than anything else a moral fight against corruption and those countries with a surplus of Reformed Christians were less likely to be corrupt than those more tolerant within the older denominations. He has since been rightly criticized for 'the worst excesses of empirical models used on their own to try and explain complex socio-cultural phenomena',[2] but others have also taken up the question of the possible contributory role of religion. North and Gwin also show that Protestantism equates to a higher respect for the rule of law, with a resulting disdain for corrupt practices.[3] Countries where Orthodox Christianity, Hinduism or Islam dominate tend to exhibit the opposite attitude towards the rule of law and are consequently more corrupt. In the case of Orthodox countries in what was formerly Eastern Europe, however, it is unclear how and if the legacy of communism affects the prevalence of corruption more than the particular or cultural expression of Christian faith.

Inspired by an analysis of the Corruption Perceptions Index (see pp. 147–51), as in Paldam's case, Douglas Beets, a Moravian professor of accounting, has more recently come to the conclusion that the least corrupt countries are those without any dominant religion, though Israel is the exception with the least corrupt religion, Judaism.[4] Less corruption arises in 'secular' situations where citizens view religion as less important, or where religious freedom is strongly respected. This is usually the case in countries where Christians make up the majority population, and where Muslims are relatively few. Where religion is not separated from public life, and religious freedom is restricted, corruption tends to thrive, as in many Muslim countries. Again, these findings will probably be questioned by many but are not made without reference to an emerging research base. Danila Serra, an economist at the University of Oxford, seems to have partially anticipated Beets' work, having used a 'global sensitivity' analytical model and found corruption to be 'lower in richer countries, where democratic institutions have been preserved for a long continuous period, and the population is mainly Protestant'.[5]

The above claims as to the ostensible Protestant advantage against the onslaught of corruption raise further questions about how churches characteristically conduct themselves in relation to the state in countries where 'children of the Reformation' mostly make up the citizenry. If the Protestant ethic encourages the formation of a more egalitarian society, how robust are its fundamentals when governments abuse their power or when 'reverse corruption' (bribery) is routinely tolerated, and in some cases, expected and tax deductible? This was reportedly the case in a modern Protestant democracy like Germany for many years until the turn of the last century.

The recognition by the Vatican in 2007 that only in the last 15 years has awareness of corruption grown at the international level is welcome but also disturbing.[6] With this has come 'the growing awareness of the need to fight it', and such a bold assertion offers hope that churches may become more responsive in future to the anti-corruption struggle being waged around the world. The lack of a solid research base among Christian academics about the potential role of churches in combating and preventing corruption is clearly something that requires attention if we wish to supplement our growing awareness. Corruption anywhere in the world cannot be willed or wished away, least of all by Christians or any faith community. This is not to suggest that the power of prayer has no relevance to the struggle; meditative recollection, demonstrated in public, of a pervasive and debilitating practice common among all cultures is itself a way of raising awareness. Prayer vigils held to focus attention on the corrupt conduct of political leaders like Robert Mugabe of Zimbabwe, who remain in office despite electoral defeat, are an effective way to unite spiritually and act collectively. If any impact is to be made by people of faith working with others, however, Christians will have to think seriously about growing their awareness of the changing nature of how corruption is manifested in society and what responses might best work. The first task is not to develop a specifically Christian contribution to a common struggle, which is what fighting corruption is, as for the sake of efficacy we have to work together with civil society organizations (like Transparency International) who have already distinguished themselves on the global stage. To join a struggle presupposes that we have adequate information about it at our disposal, and from a Christian theological perspective, this is unfortunately not the case.

Changing laws

If countries of the developing world wish to be seen to be fulfilling the requirements for good governance, as defined in most of the international conventions which we have referred to before, the formation of a new structure(s) to fight corruption will need to be taken up, as will a parallel commitment to overhauling the legislative framework, where this is necessary. Critical review and revision of legislation already in place to combat corruption, and attempts to address any shortcomings by either amending, or drafting new legislation, might be necessary. While governments have been habitually slow in responding to such pressures, civil society and churches together can create a bulwark of resistance to such malaise. In the first instance, such pressure should guarantee that laws against corruption should usually be framed in terms of an Act or Acts approved by Parliament. Such Act(s) must avoid too narrow a definition of corruption.[7] Corruption defined as 'the giving, offering, or agreeing to offer a benefit to an official or agent and the receiving, obtaining or agreeing to receive or attempting to obtain a benefit by a public official or agent' might not suffice.[8] Exactly what constitutes a benefit here is unclear, though the intention is to outlaw any kind of favour of whatever nature, financial or otherwise, that is not legally due. Two parties are identified – the corruptor and the corruptee – and it is their giving and receiving of undue benefit that is prohibited but, importantly, only where such acts 'fall within an official's or agent's strict sphere of duty'.[9] The basic problem with the above definition is that in attempting to suppress corruption, it abolishes the common law crime of bribery while narrowing the ambit of the law instead of widening it.[10]

It may also be asked why a prohibition would apply only when corruption involved a compromise in one's sphere of duty, thus making detection and prosecution quite difficult. Corrupt activities can all too easily be moved beyond one's sphere of duty in order to bypass the law, and one must assume that this has often been done. Bribery is often deemed to be illegal only if it is shown to have taken place while an official or agent exercised his or her power wrongfully. The law framed in this way will clearly be an ineffective instrument in securing successful prosecutions. When the reach of the law is of such limited range, offenders end up being charged with alternative crimes such as fraud and theft. In trying to improve the legal framework, more harm than good can be done if the imperative of devising new legislation redefining corruption (rather than making amendments to an existing Act) is ignored.

In view of the international best practice laws that are increasingly being adopted to control corruption in places such as Hong Kong, Singapore, Malaysia and India, it is quite unnecessary to begin any legislative review in a legal vacuum.[11] The provisions of the Nigerian Corrupt Practices and Other Related Offences Act of 2000 served as a basis for drawing up the new legislation in South Africa. The most immediate challenge involved the reinstatement of the common law crime of bribery. Managers in the public and private sectors are now required to blow the whistle on corruption, as failure to do so can result in a penalty of up to ten years' imprisonment. Private-to-private forms of corruption and illegal transfers of private capital are included, as are corrupt activities related to tendering and procurement. The new Corruption Act requires the Minister of Finance to keep a 'blacklist' of companies debarred from government tenders, which is open for public scrutiny.[12] Public officials showing evidence of 'unexplained wealth' are obliged to be transparent about their additional sources of income when necessary. The maximum penalty for engaging in corrupt activities is now life imprisonment. Corruption involving sporting events and the sanction of elected officials who are involved in corrupt practices are covered by the new legislation.

Despite the substantial changes, the most notable omission in the South African Act is a clause regulating party political funding, or declaring when and how such activity amounts to corrupt behaviour. Nonetheless, that South Africa has created a new legal framework for the prosecution of corrupt individuals, something which proved quite cumbersome in the past, gives the criminal justice system ample ammunition to pursue cases of corruption with much more ease than before. If good governance is about the proper exercise of social, political, economic and administrative authority to manage a country's affairs, churches cannot stand back in ignorance about the need for legal measures to remedy a deteriorating situation. Citizens, especially through civil society networks, will usually interact among themselves and with the public sector to address the prevalence of corruption. Churches can choose to watch the game from the sidelines, or by believing that their faith has practical application for reforming society, avoid eschewing their potential role in bringing about change, even in the legal environment.

A general feeling of helplessness in the face of a monolithic evil is what confronts most in the developing world. This has led some commentators to call for fundamentalist movements of a puritanical tendency to bring about a reform of public morals. Such calls are made in the belief that political elites are not capable of self-reformation or ruling in the public interest. People experience a sense of schizophrenia about public duty where, supposedly, it is said that everyone 'is sincerely in favour of respecting the public domain, and wants the bureaucracy to be at the service of the citizens, but everyone participates by means of everyday actions in the reproduction of the system he denounces'.[13] Is it then true that in Africa leaders deserve special favours and benefits (over and above the law) because they are an embodiment of what their citizens aspire to? Or, if we are to go along with a common Brazilian saying, *'Para os amigos, tudo; para os inimigos, a lei'* (Anything for friends; for enemies, the law), that the uneven application of laws against corruption (where they exist or where they are enforced) may be as much a problem as the lack of confidence in the law? In strong collectivist or family cultures, shame and guilt function differently than in western liberal democratic cultures which place emphasis on individual punishment for those who transgress the moral imperatives of society. If punishment is to be framed in group terms, with the guilty person's relationship to society affected by him being shamed, the possibility of stronger social control (of human behaviour) is apparently enhanced. Again, it does little if churches sit back in the midst of such debates about what might or might not be the most effective legal remedies for an age-old problem.

Blowing the whistle

Democratic constitutions around the world, especially those which include a Bill of Rights, would normally, among other rights, guarantee everyone the right of access to any information held by the state and to any information held by another person and which is required for the exercise or protection of rights.[14] Of course, one assumes that national legislation must be enacted to give effect to these rights where they do not exist. It might be incumbent upon churches seeking to join the fight against corruption to 'promote open and transparent democracy, foster a culture of corporate and government accountability, and assist people to realize their human rights, through supporting the effective implementation of laws which enable access to and disclosure of information'.[15] Open democracy requires both the private and public sectors to adopt a proactive 'right to know' approach, where as much information as is in the public interest is released to prevent the need for adjudicated requests. Because this right of access is so basic to the human rights regime in democratic countries, it has 'horizontal' (person-to-person) application for individual citizens, and for community organizations as well. However, in the developing world, except when a culture of open democracy is tolerated and promoted, citizens may find themselves facing insurmountable hurdles in attempting to obtain access to information. Churches, together with their civil society partners, will therefore be challenged to help create a political climate for such democratic expectations to flourish before they attempt, through parliamentary or judicial channels, to address individual requests for assistance.

The promotion of access to information is a very significant ingredient of democratic culture because 'it represents an unprecedented experiment and a unique opportunity to impose accountability through transparency in relation to both public and private power'.[16] If 'weak companies and bad governments need secrecy to survive' and if such secrecy allows for 'inefficiency, wastefulness and corruption to thrive', ordinary citizens will have a particular interest in using access to information to their advantage.[17] However, while the right of access to information in an open democratic society might be guaranteed on paper, the bureaucratic procedure to be followed might involve the possibility of lengthy delays in the granting of such access. Furthermore, if one's request is denied, the only course of appeal can be to a High Court, where considerations of cost, time and accessibility would easily serve to deter the ordinary citizen. For many, though, the 'speedy enactment' of legislation fostering greater transparency, whistle-blowing and accountability in all sectors of government business is long overdue. Public officials who pride themselves on observing confidentiality are usually the ones most threatened. Yet, as Transparency International observes, 'the intro- duction of access to information policies can increase the quality of administration significantly. Such policies foster a public sector ethic of "service to the public", enhance job satisfaction and raise the esteem in which public servants are held by the communities they serve and in which they live.'[18]

To foster greater transparency and accountability and to inculcate a culture of 'blowing the whistle' on corruption, other pieces of le- gislation should also be contemplated. Numerous countries making the transition to democracy since the fall of the Berlin Wall are try- ing to unravel their secretive past and make their administrative systems more accessible to the public. Throughout the world citizens have become more assertive about their right to know what gov- ernments are doing and how public resources are allocated.[19] In South Africa, citizens have devised ways through research projects of ensuring civil society participation in the national budgetary process, believing that 'an open budgetary process serves both to detect and prevent corruption, and to ensure that spending policies respond to public needs'.[20] But the reluctance of individuals to report acts of corruption that they have been witness to, or had knowledge of, is a basic reason that action against corruption may be slow. People have often felt intimidated, usually for fear of reprisals, about blowing the whistle on corrupt activity. During apartheid South Africa inform- ants would sometimes report on their comrades to the authorities, but when found out, were often murdered by having a burning tyre thrown around their necks. Personal obligations to members of one's extended family usually counted for more than the impersonal obligations due to the state, for which, after 1994, there was still no guarantee of legal protection or support if one blew the whistle. The fear of victimization loomed too large for ordinary citizens to take the risk, particularly in the wake of a few scandals where whistle-blowers suffered by being forced to resign their jobs.[21]

Even when whistle-blowers are offered protection, and make their disclosures in terms of the Corruption Act, the dilemma faced is no less burdensome, as the experience of Victoria Johnson illustrates. She worked as a lawyer for the City of Cape Town and blew the whistle on political corruption in the mayoral office, involving the renaming of two famous streets on spurious grounds of mass public support. Her act is said to have helped 'establish new standards of accountable governance in the Western Cape'.[22] Yet by her own account, Victoria Johnson continues to 'feel a deep sense of ambiguity' over what she did, as 'her memory of the time is always tinged with an underlying sense of discomfort and shame'.[23]

The costs and benefits calculation is as relevant for whistle-blowing as it was for other anti-corruption measures discussed earlier. Thus, in the Australian context, a challenge is made that 'the benefits of protecting those who blow the whistle on corruption and of any subsequent attempt to rout out the corruption must be balanced with the costs of such an exercise'.[24] These costs would include those to a whistle-blower such as Victoria Johnson whose decision to act may be avenged; 'the cost to any individual improperly or wrongly accused by a whistle-blower; the cost to the organization involved; and the cost to society of the investigation which may follow'.[25] It remains to be seen whether a new workplace culture of whistle-blowing, one that can have a powerful deterrent effect against corruption (public benefit), can supplant the fear and personal risks (human cost) usually attached to it, and whether governments can afford the attendant monetary costs. For churches, though, the question might not be so much about costs as about the principle. To what extent can church communities join with civil society, business and government in promoting 'open democracy' when their own culture of closet theocracy might be in conflict? Church leaders hold sacred office and are expected to uphold values of justice, accountability and transparency, but the extent to which they comply with the expectations of public scrutiny is not always clear. It is surely not a feature of church culture that fellow workers are expected or encouraged to 'spy' on each others' conduct and report breaches to their bishop.

It is almost as if developing countries are required to muddle their way through to fulfilling a set of requirements which more often than not might not be culturally sensitive. Where a country's laws, especially new ones ostensibly introduced to comply with international demands, are not adequately thought through they will leave citizens with a sense of ambiguity. Consider the innumerable cases where corrupt leaders enjoy virtual impunity and are, as a rule, spared prosecution. Often, even after being found guilty, the culprit is simply relieved of his duties, which is not much of an incentive to someone to blow the whistle on his misdemeanour. It is not that there is a lack of moral repugnance; there will be debate and anger at the local level, but this will be managed 'in-house' without neighbours or outsiders becoming involved. To incur the scorn of society for exposing a friend or colleague for devious behaviour is too high a price for many, not least those who might gather for prayer on a Sunday.

In the words of one pessimistic observer, Olivier de Sardan, 'the effect of acquired habits and the normalization of commonplace practices renders the situation more or less irreversible'.[26] For him, corruption is always seen by an individual as someone else's problem, for the logic of solidarity networks in Africa is 'so rigorous that anyone who fails to respect his obligations to a member of one of the networks to which he belongs suffers reproach'.[27] He furthermore claims that societal pressures are strongly inclined towards the accumulation of personal wealth, which in turn is expected to bring benefits to the wider family. Rivalry, or jealousy, then becomes a positive force, spurring one on to improve one's economic situation and social status. Christianity in Africa has been spreading rapidly, especially via Pentecostal-type churches preaching a prosperity-type gospel that encourages wealth creation among their members. While the coincidence might not be so obvious to some, it must be incumbent upon churches to examine the moral assumptions within their theologies that may help or hinder the spread of corruption. The challenge is even more pronounced when governments are seeking to frame a battery of laws to regulate practices which qualify as cultural for some but corrupt for others.

Speaking out

One of the foremost media critics of apartheid, Allister Sparks, wrote in 1988 that his greatest fear for South Africa's future was more about corruption than the dismantling of apartheid. He described it as 'the cancer of Africa, the malignancy that seemed to grow exponentially throughout our continent, bringing debilitation and death to country after country'.[28] By 1995 he felt 'confirmed in that view' and consequently called for a 'campaign against corruption' to prevent the 'great South African experiment' in democracy from failing.[29] As we noticed earlier, the media forms an integral pillar of the national integrity system and was also effectively used to change public perceptions and promote the successes of the ICAC in Hong Kong. The importance attached to the role of the media in fighting corruption should likewise not be overlooked, as the media can support and work together with government in creating a sustained campaign to highlight the causes of corruption and offer solutions for its reduction. The necessity for an independent media to report freely on acts of corruption is obviously in the public interest and should not be taken for granted in every context.

Often, unlike other aspects of a national strategy, public confidence is boosted via the media thanks to the reporting efforts of individual journalists who have exposed numerous, often suppressed, cases of corruption. It has been said of independent-minded investigative journalists that simply by doing their jobs well, they have for many years played a central role in promoting democracy, good governance and global awareness of corruption.[30] When media efforts to expose corruption fail to materialize, this is often due to the lack of corporate will for such action, or possibly to the lack of resources. Either way, it is a peculiar challenge for officials even of progressive governments to work with and support journalists intent on upholding the freedom and independence of the media. Tensions around this media 'space' will generally abound, with government officials wary of being seen as overtly critical of the ruling party, or the presidency in particular, most of the time.[31] Civil servants are after all employed to serve the government of the day, but as a day can last a decade or more in places like Zimbabwe or Burma, blowing the whistle within the systems of government operations can be risky. If an official goes to the media to blow the whistle on a politician, he or she should not automatically be punished for having technically deviated from the prescribed procedure of whistle-blowing as might be laid out in law. Sometimes the structures of government are not fully functional or have not yet developed into political maturity, leaving space for journalists valuably to fill the gap, especially while democratic institutions are being built up;

journalists can play a vital role in ensuring that good governance and accountability are achieved.[32] A compact between government and the media to 'work together' in exposing corruption might therefore be more difficult to create than the national strategy suggests.

As mentioned above, the media has historically played an important role in exposing corruption but its watchdog status can be compromised through lack of resources. If media enterprises remain underfunded, they can easily fall prey to large advertisers who exert a powerful controlling interest in the media companies. The threat that monopolies will arise is one that must be fiercely resisted. A handful of groups often control nearly all newspapers in any given country in the developing world, while few privately owned broadcasters are licensed to operate alongside the public broadcaster.[33] The ownership of the media companies will be irrelevant if journalists 'demonstrate their independence, objectivity and professionalism each and every day in order to earn public trust and confidence'.[34] Yet, as Transparency International believes, 'it is imperative that the owners of the media ensure that journalists are paid wages which encourage independence, rather than dependence'.[35] Serious investigative reporting, which can carry high risks, involving legal challenges and loss of life, is often time-consuming and costly, but remains pivotal to providing the public with relevant coverage on corruption cases. The ability of the media to shape public attitudes and government policy is often underestimated, hence the view that it is not only useful for raising public awareness 'but it can also contribute by providing the necessary support of the civil society to government's anti-corruption initiatives'.[36]

Moreover, as noted in the UN *Anti-Corruption Tool Kit*, 'journalists, editors and newspaper owners can take on an active role in combating corruption by facilitating public debate on the need to introduce anti-corruption policies and measures'.[37] The adoption of such a role would serve to counteract the concern that journalists are often put under pressure to report the 'right angle' by those implicated in corruption and other interest groups.[38] Greater support for efforts to build the capacity of journalists so that they report responsibly on corruption-related cases must as a rule be encouraged.[39] But 'such training in investigative journalism will be a wasted effort if the media is not free and independent of political influence and if access to information is not sufficiently guaranteed'.[40] The case of Mozambique's top investigative journalist, Carlos Cardoso, is worth mentioning here, as he was murdered in an ambush in 2000 for his tireless work in exposing political corruption within a faction of government involving a leading bank and an organized crime syndicate. Thus, the challenge of a media campaign in the fight against corruption might be better placed if the emphasis were to shift from 'working together' to greater access for journalists to information residing in the public sector, more especially government, and to the overcoming of resource and capacity constraints. While costs are a debilitating factor, as is possibly the lack of political will, there remains widespread recognition both for the value of a media campaign against corruption and for the development of a plan for the implementation of such a campaign.

Of course, if churches are to contribute to public efforts for a free and independent press (something of high value but absent in many parts of the world), they will be indirectly facilitating the creation of a political and social environment for the unhindered reporting of corrupt activities. Catholic Bishops' Conferences have led the way in the Philippines and many parts of Latin America, subjecting corporate greed and political graft to scathing criticism which then gets reported when its statements are 'newsworthy'. In view of the very nature of corruption, and its peculiar character of almost always replicating itself, it behoves Christians to engage the media in speaking out even when it may be capable of doing little else. To articulate moral truth in the face of screaming injustice is after all the prophetic duty and calling of the churches. When the values of transparency and accountability are being trampled upon by corrupt governments who notoriously restrict press freedom, often the only competing source of authority rests with church leaders who can and should act in solidarity with those silenced.

Moral regeneration

If churches join civil society organizations to address the collapse of the moral order of society, they can wisely contribute towards the creation of autonomous and powerful grassroots movements able to drive the rehabilitation of society's morals. Global concern about the moral decay of societies, as evidenced by spiralling crimes of murder, theft, domestic violence against women and children, and corruption, is commendable, as would be any attempt to work with religious groups to bring such matters to the nation's attention. If and when the establishment of a programme to manage the activities related to moral regeneration is contemplated, the role that government will play is something that will require careful clarification. While something like a moral regeneration campaign might be a vehicle that can be effectively used for a limited time to fight corruption, this can only be done at the level of civil society. The project of fighting corruption in the public sector is one that must be driven by governments as state authority rather than government as moral conscience of the nation, particularly when matters of law enforcement are concerned. That there usually exists a groundswell of moral outrage within governments towards many of society's ills, including corruption, is commendable provided that government does not usurp civil society's role of holding governments accountable to their citizens for their actions.

Those who have observed South Africa's struggle for democratic freedoms will agree that the tide began to turn against apartheid in the late 1980s with the imposition of economic sanctions by the international community. It was also during this time that the National Party government of Mr P. W. Botha, in attempting to repackage its oppressive ideology, requested the Dutch Reformed Church to support his new position on mixed marriages. Botha was of course intent on removing this embarrassing law from the legal statutes but he first sought the blessing of an institution that was perceived as the 'National Party at prayer'. His successor, F. W. de Klerk, similarly urged Christian churches in 1990 to 'formulate a strategy conducive to negotiation', which they did when they met en masse in Rustenburg and adopted a vision for the new South Africa. Nelson Mandela, the first democratically elected president, coined the notion of an 'RDP [Reconstruction and Development Programme] of the soul' along the lines of his political blueprint for the new South Africa. He was thus instrumental in calling religious leaders together at a Morals Summit in 1998, and in his last opening of parliament, affirmed that 'Our hope for the future depends on our resolution as a nation in dealing with the scourge of corruption'. Church and state have historically shared common interests and agendas, and in their quest for the good society, have served to inspire, quicken and even criticize each other. The contribution of faith-based organizations to fighting corruption in South Africa may also be viewed in the context of this paradigm, as the formation of the Goedgedacht Forum illustrates.

Case study: An unfinished house

Globally, traditional liberal representative politics as currently prac-
ticed seem inadequate for the consumerist, information age in which
we live. Politics where parties represented specific class interests
has dissipated to some extent as class structures have become porous
and fragmented. Rather than a battle of different interests, as Bernard
Crick described in his influential 'In Defence of Politics,' parties now
do battle largely on issues of style, presentation and personalities.
Policies based on the results of focus groups are incoherent and
largely indistinguishable across parties. Parties are trying to keep
pace with the fragmented, oft-changing views of the electors, more
and more of whom feel alienated from the political process.

The challenge for those committed to politics as the art of the
impossible is to re-energize, re-democratize the political process
in a manner that places morality at its centre, with transparent
accountability as its most crucial tool. I believe that there are certain basic global requirements for a more honest polity including:

- full disclosure of every cent [penny] of party funding, from whatever source;
- a global regulatory environment for corporations, with specific
  regimes for the arms, pharmaceutical, gambling and mineral
  and resource extraction industries;
- a global corruption watchdog that has the power to fine trans-
  gressors in the public and private sectors (both corrupters and
  corrupted) and, in the case of extreme violations, to deregister
  companies and political parties;
- a global citizens' movement with a Citizens' Charter for
  Political Parties that demands honesty, transparency and consultation at all levels of government.

(Extract from Andrew Feinstein, *After the Party*,
Johannesburg: Jonathan Ball, 2007, pp. 259–60.)

This rural initiative was founded on the back of a search for a
'values-driven', deeply democratic, prosperous, harmonious and
peaceful South Africa where it was thought possible to achieve the
'common good' by strengthening democratic, participative institutions and movements, promoting justice and peace, and addressing
the moral vacuum present in society. It was founded in the tradition

of the Catholic Church's concern for human values but remained independent of ecclesial control. The forum openly acknowledged and respected the dignity of all religions and moral traditions as well. Its methods of achieving its aims were by promoting and organizing debates on issues of national importance where human values were seen to be under threat, and by communicating the substantive outcomes of such debates as widely as possible. Topical issues addressed included moral alienation and lawlessness, racism and the media, the impact of AIDS on children, poverty reduction and fighting corruption. Its debate on corruption was opened by leading anti-corruption stalwart Judge Willem Heath in August 2000 at the forum's farm in Malmesbury, outside Cape Town. The forum later published its insights and recommendations from this debate, including a call for more transparency and a recognition of the interface between morality and corruption. Corruption was seen as part of the wider problem of non-observance of the law. The forum accepted that if senior civil servants were bribed, business achieved undue influence in government and that much corruption was initiated by the private sector. The media, it was acknowledged, could play an important role in uncovering corruption and even in investigating it, as this would also serve as a deterrent. Fragmentation in tackling corruption within the South African government was noted because of the number of anti-corruption units that existed. State prosecuting agencies were called on to 'fry the big fish' in bringing corrupt actors to court. The forum concluded that instituting successful prosecutions in cases involving high-profile offenders would send a message to other, less prominent offenders that corruption did not pay. While it was noted that there was an Asset Register for MPs and that senior public servants were required to make financial disclosures, thus preventing conflicts of interest, these measures against corruption, it was said, needed to be strengthened. In order to combat corruption effectively, a combined commitment by the public, private and civil society sectors was also viewed as essential.

South Africa's transition to democracy in 1994 also spawned other church-based projects designed to address the challenge of rebuilding the moral fabric. The Ford Foundation initiated a process of socially transformative education by providing funding to theological faculties and schools, enabling them to engage in strategic planning for the future. This was based on the assumption that the leadership qualities of such anti-apartheid critics as Desmond Tutu, Beyers

Naudé, Stanley Mogoba, Frank Chikane, Brigalia Bam and others had been shaped by certain kinds of experiences in their theological formation which put a premium on the development and promotion of ethically sensitive leadership. The Church Community Leadership Trust (CCLT) was then established against this background with the stated goal of nurturing moral leadership for social transformation. Allied to this hope was the constant need to engage in the contextualization of theological education, which of itself led to the formation of a national initiative that in June 1996 committed itself to producing and promoting moral leadership for social transformation.

As incidents of corruption were being more frequently reported in the media, CCLT became increasingly aware of the 'crisis of moral values with a corresponding ground swell desire for responsible citizenship that is committed to a just and caring humanity'. This awareness arose with particular reference to the high levels of crime, corruption and moral disintegration. All sectors of society, including business, government, civil society, labour, education and religion, were showing signs of strain and a programme of integrity training and development was envisioned in response. Such training was to focus on promoting a high standard of ethical behaviour with strong emphasis on the values of effectiveness, transparency, accountability, probity, equity, solidarity, justice and responsible care. The National Engagement for Ethics Development (NEED) was formed as a result, a CCLT programme where the development of integrity was seen essentially as a community activity. NEED saw its task as to act as a facilitator of a process whereby 'it not only imparts knowledge about integrity, norms, values and morality, but contributes to the release of energies which create integrity and moral development'. Clearly, directly and indirectly, such an initiative offered enormous potential for the rehabilitation of values (in a country where leaders were bemoaning the breakdown of its moral fabric), with consequent effects on the struggle against corruption.

Hope for the future

When the famous French anthropologist Marcel Mauss, building on the work of his uncle Emile Durkheim, attempted to understand the form and reason for exchange in archaic society, he arrived at the following conclusion in a masterful, if dated, study:

Societies have progressed in so far as they themselves, their subgroups, and lastly, the individuals in them, have succeeded in stabilizing relationships, giving, receiving, and finally, giving in return. To trade, the first condition was to lay aside the spear. From then onwards they succeeded in exchanging goods and persons, no longer only between clans, but between tribes and nations, and, above all, between individuals. Only then did people learn how to create mutual interests, giving mutual satisfaction, and, in the end, to defend them without having to resort to arms. Thus the clan, the tribe, and peoples have learnt how to oppose and to give one another without sacrificing themselves to one another. This is what tomorrow, in our so-called civilized world, classes and nations and individuals also, must learn.[41]

With the passing of time, though, it is abundantly clear that human beings have chosen not to learn the 'rules' of living at peace and in harmony with each other, neither as nations nor as communities. We give and we receive, we exchange our gifts and wares, we trade all too often in the absence of norms such as mutual interest and mutual satisfaction. Corruption, as the subversion of this civil basis for human co-existence, and a denial of the mutuality principle of life, as a consequence appears destined endlessly to tarnish our lives. To make such a check with reality is not to be cynical or accept defeat in the struggle against the practice and prevalence of corruption, however; it is to accept that government decisions can too often be bought or sold, that only a minority of the political bribes paid each year are to officials in the developing world, and that democracy itself is increasingly vulnerable to the power or lure of money.

Christians inspired by the same gospel, whether active or dormant members of a church, will wish to consider working with civil society to become advocates for the changing of laws and the improvement of lives. The debate about fighting corruption, as it has evolved at the empirical level, though, is overshadowed by economic arguments and the 'one-cap-fits-all' approach which puts the emphasis on law enforcement. Churches will need to relate to this reality in a creative way if their members are to make a difference and not be put off by the technocrats who have already codified the discourse. Though we agree with the call for more attempts to blow the whistle on corruption, as this is a very important step identified in most of the international conventions against corruption, this measure raises ambiguous cultural questions (about hierarchical culture too) which churches are uniquely placed to help debate. It may be premature at this stage to make pronouncements or to venture the testing of every act of exchange in terms of its propensity to increase or decrease corruption, especially with regard to what is given as a free gift. It is therefore difficult to be exactly sure about when giving to charity might or might not contribute to corruption, or when buying or boycotting a certain product might help or hinder corruption. It is much clearer, on the other hand, to assert that corruption contributes to an increase in poverty and a violation of human rights. The dearth of expertise on measures to fight corruption within Christian institutions should challenge us to overcome the knowledge deficit and create space for prophetic engagement around something that is a blight on societies everywhere.

Of course, it must be a cause for celebration that religion has been put back into the public square and that those who wear its badge cannot any longer watch from the sidelines. The point of this book, the like of which is unlikely to have been written two decades ago when the word corruption was used only with restraint, is that Christian faith has serious practical implications for the reform of society. Christians, by engaging or immersing themselves in a struggle against corruption, will by implication be rejecting a political doctrine that excludes religion from the conduct of public affairs. The public square has been and continues to be quite 'naked', bereft of faith-based initiatives which give voice with moral authority to the need for greater transparency and accountability from our leaders. Ours is a time for the 'deprivatization' of religion, where civic life can once again recapture its vocal verve by setting the public agenda, lest the public have it made up by the media's flashy tabloids or 'spun' by vote-seeking politicians. Amid the 'noise of solemn assemblies' about their own decline, it might appear far-fetched to imagine churches being involved with other formations, let alone being in the forefront of a global struggle which has to compete with other legitimate, sometimes more urgent, campaigns and civil society initiatives. It is possible that our fatalistic or inert disposition to the disease we call corruption was in the past nurtured mostly by our lack of knowledge of it, partly by our limited capacity to work towards its elimination, and in some cases by our own complicity, or simply because it was the way things got done or was the way of life as we saw it. That time is now thankfully past.

Appendix
The Corruption Perceptions Index

(Source: Transparency International)

The Corruption Perceptions Index (CPI) was first released in 1995 by Transparency International as a tool to measure perceived levels of corruption among public officials in 41 countries of the world. That number has now risen to 180, and the task of preparing the CPI has become much more elaborate, with more polls and surveys being used to arrive at the respective country scores. Countries which score higher are the ones perceived to be less corrupt; a lower score in comparison is indicative of higher (perceived) levels of corruption. It remains far from clear as to what is actually being measured by the CPI, for if corruption is mostly hidden, how can it be measured at all? Still, despite lingering doubts about the reliability of its data and the fact that scores cannot be changed overnight, it remains widely used and offers a glimpse of the world map of corruption. It assumes, like its founder, Professor Johann Graf Lambsdorff of the University of Passau, Germany, that corruption amounts to a misuse of public office for private benefit and that countries can, over time, take action to improve public perception and score higher on the index. Leaders of many developing countries have in the past expressed misgivings about the usefulness of a measurement tool such as the CPI, which appears to inevitably favour the developed world.

Country rank	Country	2008 CPI score	Surveys used	Confidence range
1	Denmark	9.3	6	9.1–9.4
1	New Zealand	9.3	6	9.2–9.5
1	Sweden	9.3	6	9.2–9.4
4	Singapore	9.2	9	9.0–9.3
5	Finland	9.0	6	8.4–9.4
5	Switzerland	9.0	6	8.7–9.2
7	Iceland	8.9	5	8.1–9.4
7	Netherlands	8.9	6	8.5–9.1
9	Australia	8.7	8	8.2–9.1
9	Canada	8.7	6	8.4–9.1

Country rank	Country	2008 CPI score	Surveys used	Confidence range
11	Luxembourg	8.3	6	7.8–8.8
12	Austria	8.1	6	7.6–8.6
12	Hong Kong	8.1	8	7.5–8.6
14	Germany	7.9	6	7.5–8.2
14	Norway	7.9	6	7.5–8.3
16	Ireland	7.7	6	7.5–7.9
16	United Kingdom	7.7	6	7.2–8.1
18	Belgium	7.3	6	7.2–7.4
18	Japan	7.3	8	7.0–7.6
18	USA	7.3	8	6.7–7.7
21	Saint Lucia	7.1	3	6.6–7.3
22	Barbados	7.0	4	6.5–7.3
23	Chile	6.9	7	6.5–7.2
23	France	6.9	6	6.5–7.3
23	Uruguay	6.9	5	6.5–7.2
26	Slovenia	6.7	8	6.5–7.0
27	Estonia	6.6	8	6.2–6.9
28	Qatar	6.5	4	5.6–7.0
28	Saint Vincent and the Grenadines	6.5	3	4.7–7.3
28	Spain	6.5	6	5.7–6.9
31	Cyprus	6.4	3	5.9–6.8
32	Portugal	6.1	6	5.6–6.7
33	Dominica	6.0	3	4.7–6.8
33	Israel	6.0	6	5.6–6.3
35	United Arab Emirates	5.9	5	4.8–6.8
36	Botswana	5.8	6	5.2–6.4
36	Malta	5.8	4	5.3–6.3
36	Puerto Rico	5.8	4	5.0–6.6
39	Taiwan	5.7	9	5.4–6.0
40	South Korea	5.6	9	5.1–6.3
41	Mauritius	5.5	5	4.9–6.4
41	Oman	5.5	5	4.5–6.4
43	Bahrain	5.4	5	4.3–5.9
43	Macao	5.4	4	3.9–6.2
45	Bhutan	5.2	5	4.5–5.9
45	Czech Republic	5.2	8	4.8–5.9
47	Cape Verde	5.1	3	3.4–5.6
47	Costa Rica	5.1	5	4.8–5.3
47	Hungary	5.1	8	4.8–5.4
47	Jordan	5.1	7	4.0–6.2
47	Malaysia	5.1	9	4.5–5.7
52	Latvia	5.0	6	4.8–5.2
52	Slovakia	5.0	8	4.5–5.3

Country rank	Country	2008 CPI score	Surveys used	Confidence range
54	South Africa	4.9	8	4.5–5.1
55	Italy	4.8	6	4.0–5.5
55	Seychelles	4.8	4	3.7–5.9
57	Greece	4.7	6	4.2–5.0
58	Lithuania	4.6	8	4.1–5.2
58	Poland	4.6	8	4.0–5.2
58	Turkey	4.6	7	4.1–5.1
61	Namibia	4.5	6	3.8–5.1
62	Croatia	4.4	8	4.0–4.8
62	Samoa	4.4	3	3.4–4.8
62	Tunisia	4.4	6	3.5–5.5
65	Cuba	4.3	4	3.6–4.8
65	Kuwait	4.3	5	3.3–5.2
67	El Salvador	3.9	5	3.2–4.5
67	Georgia	3.9	7	3.2–4.6
67	Ghana	3.9	6	3.4–4.5
70	Colombia	3.8	7	3.3–4.5
70	Romania	3.8	8	3.4–4.2
72	Bulgaria	3.6	8	3.0–4.3
72	China	3.6	9	3.1–4.3
72	Macedonia (Former Yugoslav Republic of)	3.6	6	2.9–4.3
72	Mexico	3.6	7	3.4–3.9
72	Peru	3.6	6	3.4–4.1
72	Suriname	3.6	4	3.3–4.0
72	Swaziland	3.6	4	2.9–4.3
72	Trinidad and Tobago	3.6	4	3.1–4.0
80	Brazil	3.5	7	3.2–4.0
80	Burkina Faso	3.5	7	2.9–4.2
80	Morocco	3.5	6	3.0–4.0
80	Saudi Arabia	3.5	5	3.0–3.9
80	Thailand	3.5	9	3.0–3.9
85	Albania	3.4	5	3.3–3.4
85	India	3.4	10	3.2–3.6
85	Madagascar	3.4	7	2.8–4.0
85	Montenegro	3.4	5	2.5–4.0
85	Panama	3.4	5	2.8–3.7
85	Senegal	3.4	7	2.9–4.0
85	Serbia	3.4	6	3.0–4.0
92	Algeria	3.2	6	2.9–3.4
92	Bosnia and Herzegovina	3.2	7	2.9–3.5
92	Lesotho	3.2	5	2.3–3.8
92	Sri Lanka	3.2	7	2.9–3.5
96	Benin	3.1	6	2.8–3.4

Country rank	Country	2008 CPI score	Surveys used	Confidence range
96	Gabon	3.1	4	2.8–3.3
96	Guatemala	3.1	5	2.3–4.0
96	Jamaica	3.1	5	2.8–3.3
96	Kiribati	3.1	3	2.5–3.4
96	Mali	3.1	6	2.8–3.3
102	Bolivia	3.0	6	2.8–3.2
102	Djibouti	3.0	4	2.2–3.3
102	Dominican Republic	3.0	5	2.7–3.2
102	Lebanon	3.0	4	2.2–3.6
102	Mongolia	3.0	7	2.6–3.3
102	Rwanda	3.0	5	2.7–3.2
102	Tanzania	3.0	7	2.5–3.3
109	Argentina	2.9	7	2.5–3.3
109	Armenia	2.9	7	2.6–3.1
109	Belize	2.9	3	1.8–3.7
109	Moldova	2.9	7	2.4–3.7
109	Solomon Islands	2.9	3	2.5–3.2
109	Vanuatu	2.9	3	2.5–3.2
115	Egypt	2.8	6	2.4–3.2
115	Malawi	2.8	6	2.4–3.1
115	Maldives	2.8	4	1.7–4.3
115	Mauritania	2.8	7	2.2–3.7
115	Niger	2.8	6	2.4–3.0
115	Zambia	2.8	7	2.5–3.0
121	Nepal	2.7	6	2.4–3.0
121	Nigeria	2.7	7	2.3–3.0
121	São Tomé and Príncipe	2.7	3	2.1–3.1
121	Togo	2.7	6	1.9–3.7
121	Vietnam	2.7	9	2.4–3.1
126	Eritrea	2.6	5	1.7–3.6
126	Ethiopia	2.6	7	2.2–2.9
126	Guyana	2.6	4	2.4–2.7
126	Honduras	2.6	6	2.3–2.9
126	Indonesia	2.6	10	2.3–2.9
126	Libya	2.6	5	2.2–3.0
126	Mozambique	2.6	7	2.4–2.9
126	Uganda	2.6	7	2.2–3.0
134	Comoros	2.5	3	1.9–3.0
134	Nicaragua	2.5	6	2.2–2.7
134	Pakistan	2.5	7	2.0–2.8
134	Ukraine	2.5	8	2.2–2.8
138	Liberia	2.4	4	1.8–2.8
138	Paraguay	2.4	5	2.0–2.7
138	Tonga	2.4	3	1.9–2.6

Country rank	Country	2008 CPI score	Surveys used	Confidence range
141	Cameroon	2.3	7	2.0–2.7
141	Iran	2.3	4	1.9–2.5
141	Philippines	2.3	9	2.1–2.5
141	Yemen	2.3	5	1.9–2.8
145	Kazakhstan	2.2	6	1.8–2.7
145	Timor-Leste (East Timor)	2.2	4	1.8–2.5
147	Bangladesh	2.1	7	1.7–2.4
147	Kenya	2.1	7	1.9–2.4
147	Russia	2.1	8	1.9–2.5
147	Syria	2.1	5	1.6–2.4
151	Belarus	2.0	5	1.6–2.5
151	Central African Republic	2.0	5	1.9–2.2
151	Côte d'Ivoire	2.0	6	1.7–2.5
151	Ecuador	2.0	5	1.8–2.2
151	Laos	2.0	6	1.6–2.3
151	Papua New Guinea	2.0	6	1.6–2.3
151	Tajikistan	2.0	8	1.7–2.3
158	Angola	1.9	6	1.5–2.2
158	Azerbaijan	1.9	8	1.7–2.1
158	Burundi	1.9	6	1.5–2.3
158	Congo, Republic	1.9	6	1.8–2.0
158	Gambia	1.9	5	1.5–2.4
158	Guinea-Bissau	1.9	3	1.8–2.0
158	Sierra Leone	1.9	5	1.8–2.0
158	Venezuela	1.9	7	1.8–2.0
166	Cambodia	1.8	7	1.7–1.9
166	Kyrgyzstan	1.8	7	1.7–1.9
166	Turkmenistan	1.8	5	1.5–2.2
166	Uzbekistan	1.8	8	1.5–2.2
166	Zimbabwe	1.8	7	1.5–2.1
171	Congo, Democratic Republic	1.7	6	1.6–1.9
171	Equatorial Guinea	1.7	4	1.5–1.8
173	Chad	1.6	6	1.5–1.7
173	Guinea	1.6	6	1.3–1.9
173	Sudan	1.6	6	1.5–1.7
176	Afghanistan	1.5	4	1.1–1.6
177	Haiti	1.4	4	1.1–1.7
178	Iraq	1.3	4	1.1–1.6
178	Myanmar	1.3	4	1.0–1.5
180	Somalia	1.0	4	0.5–1.4

Notes

Introduction

1 The only text of note has been written in German. See Karl Rennstich 1990, *Korruption: Eine Herausforderung für Gesellschaft und Kirche*, Stuttgart: Quell.

2 C. Frankfort-Nachmias and D. Nachmias 1992, *Research Methods in the Social Sciences*, Sevenoaks, Kent: Edward Arnold, p. 46.

3 Ibid., pp. 44–6, where Thomas Smith's 'standard' model is discussed in more detail.

4 See, for example, J. Pope (ed.) 1996, *National Integrity Systems: The TI Source Book*, Berlin: Transparency International, and 2000, *Anti-Corruption in Transition: A Contribution to a Policy Debate*, Washington DC: World Bank.

5 Danila Serra 2006, 'Empirical Determinants of Corruption: A Sensitivity Analysis', in *Public Choice* 126, 225–56.

6 J. P. Oliver de Sardan 1999, 'A Moral Economy of Corruption in Africa', in *The Journal of Modern African Studies* 37:1, pp. 25–52.

7 T. L. Saaty 1990, *The Analytic Hierarchy Process: Planning, Priority Setting, Resource Allocation*, Pittsburgh, PA: University of Pittsburgh, RWS Publications.

1 The problem with corruption

1 The most widely accepted legal instrument on the subject of corruption, ostensibly drafted for the sake of its elimination or control, and approved by the United Nations General Assembly, resists any attempt to offer such a definition. See United Nations Convention Against Corruption (2003).

2 One of the more useful texts to cover the discussion on definitions is A. J. Heidenheimer (ed.) 1970, *Political Corruption: Readings in Comparative Analyses*, New Brunswick, NJ: Transaction Books, pp. 3–64.

3 M. U. Ekpo (ed.) 1979, *Bureaucratic Corruption in Sub-Saharan Africa: Towards a Search for Causes and Consequences*, Washington DC: University Press of America, p. 1.

4 Heidenheimer *Political Corruption*, p. 4.

5 P. Hodgkinson 1997, 'The Sociology of Corruption – Some Themes and Issues', *Sociology* 31:1, 19.

6 J. Gardiner 1993, 'Defining Corruption, Coping with Corruption in a Borderless World', in M. Punch, E. Kolthoff, K. van der Vijer and B. van Vliet (eds), *Proceedings of the Fifth International Anti-Corruption Conference*, Deventer, Netherlands: Kluwer, p. 26.

7 *Encyclopaedia of the Social Sciences.* Vol. IV, 1930–1935, New York: Macmillan Co., p. 449.

8 M. Robinson 1998, 'Corruption and Development: An Introduction', in M. Robinson (ed.), *Corruption and Development*, London: Frank Cass, p. 3.

9 J. G. Lambsdorff, 'Corruption and the Underground Economy', draft copy of paper prepared for publication in forthcoming *Encyclopedia of Globalization* and distributed at a seminar on economics of corruption held in Passua, Germany, in October 2003.

10 M. K. Khan 1996, 'A Typology of Corrupt Transactions in Developing Countries', *IDS Bulletin* 27:2, 12.

11 Ibid.

12 Ibid., p. 14.

13 H. Alatas 1991, *Corruption: Its Nature, Causes and Functions*, Kuala Lumpur: S. Abdul Majeed & Co, p. 141.

14 Ibid.

15 Lambsdorff, 'Corruption and the Underground Economy'.

16 S. Rose-Ackerman 1999, *Corruption and Government: Causes, Consequences and Reform*, Cambridge: Cambridge University Press, p. 145.

17 R. Williams 2003, 'Political Corruption in the United States', in M. J. Bull and J. L. Newell 2003, *Corruption in Contemporary Politics*, Houndmills, Hampshire: Palgrave Macmillan, p. 68.

18 Lambsdorff, 'Corruption and the Underground Economy'.

19 Rose-Ackerman, *Corruption and Government*, p. 226.

20 J. M. Mbaku 1998, 'Bureaucratic and Political Corruption in Africa', in *Corruption and the Crisis of Institutional Reforms in Africa*, Lewiston, NY: Edwin Mellen Press, p. 53.

21 Ibid.

22 Ibid.

23 R. Williams 2003, *Political Corruption in Africa*, Aldershot, Hampshire: Gower, p. 42.

24 Ibid., p. 43.

25 Ibid., p. 47.

26 Ibid.

27 V. Samuel 1998, 'Business and Corruption', in B. J. van der Walt, W. A. S. Cornelis and V. Samuel (eds), *Corruption*, Potchefstroom University, p. 10.

28 S. van der Merwe 2001, *Combat Corruption Collectively: Mobilizing South African Civil Society on Corruption, Governance and Ethics*, Pretoria: Van Schaik, pp. 9–13.

29 J. Girling 1997, *Corruption, Capitalism and Democracy*, London: Routledge, p. 4.

30 Ibid., p. 8.

31 V. Tanzi 2002, 'Corruption Around the World: Causes, Consequences, Scope, and Cures', in G. T. Abed and S. Gupta (eds), *Governance,*

Corruption and Economic Performance, Washington DC: International Monetary Fund, p. 38.

32 P. Mauro 1995, 'Corruption and Growth', *Quarterly Journal of Economics* CX.3 (August), 681–712.

33 Lambsdorff, 'Corruption and the Underground Economy'.

34 L. W. J. C. Huberts 1996, 'Expert Views on Public Corruption Around the Globe: Research Report on the Views of an International Expert Panel', Amsterdam: PSPA Publications, p. 36. A similar approach to measuring perceptions of corruption by expert group consultation was advocated by Richard Holloway for application in particular geographical settings. See 'Scoring Perceptions in Other Fields: Analogies for Measuring Perceptions of Corruption', unpublished paper delivered at IIPE Workshop on Measuring Corruption, Brisbane, Australia, 4–7 October 2002.

35 Center for Public Integrity, press release, 25 June 2004. See <www.publicintegrity.org>.

36 Ibid.

37 D. Kaufmann, A. Kraay and M. Mastruzzi 2003, 'Governance Matters III: Governance Indicators for 1996–2002', draft World Bank paper.

38 Edward L. Cleary 2007, 'New Priority for Churches and Missions: Combating Corruption', *International Bulletin of Missionary Research*, 31:4 (October), 184.

39 Reports of the WCC Eighth Assembly, December 1998. See <www.wcc-coe.org/wcc/assembly/index>.

40 Cleary, 'New Priority for Churches', p. 183.

41 R. E. Davies and E. G. Rupp (eds) 1965, *A History of the Methodist Church in Great Britain*, Vol. I, London: Epworth, p. 65.

42 Mark Zirnsak, Kerryn Clarke and Annie Feith, *From Corruption to Good Governance*, United Church in Australia, Victoria and Tasmania, March 2008, p. 24.

43 Statement on the Fight Against Corruption, Pontifical Council for Justice and Peace, 2–3 June 2006, Vatican, Rome, <http://www.vatican.va/roman_curia/pontifical_councils/justpeace/documents/rc_pc_ju>.

2 When and why corruption happens

1 *The Economist*, 15 June 1957.

2 Eric McKitrick 1956, 'The Study of Corruption', in Ekpo, *Bureaucratic Corruption*, p. 63. First read as a paper at the 33rd Annual Institute of the Society for Social Research of the University of Chicago, 1 June 1956.

3 Colin Leys 1970, 'What is the Problem about Corruption?', in Heidenheimer, *Political Corruption*, p. 31. First published in 1965 in *Journal of Modern African Studies* 3:2.

4 G. Myrdal 1970, Corruption as a Hindrance to Modernization in South Asia, in Heidenheimer, *Political Corruption*, p. 230. First published in 1968 in G. Myrdal, *Asian Drama: An Enquiry into the Poverty of Nations*. Vol. II, New York: Twentieth Century.

5　See the extensive collection of 58 essays on the subject of corruption that are reproduced in Heidenheimer, *Political Corruption*.

6　G. R. Montinola and R. W. Jackman 2002, 'Sources of Corruption: A Cross-Country Study', *British Journal of Political Science* 32:1 (January), 147.

7　R. Klitgaard 1988, *Controlling Corruption*, Berkeley: University of California Press, p. ix.

8　A. Demetrios 2001, 'The International Anti-Corruption Campaigns: Whose Ethics?', in G. E. Caiden, O. P. Dwivedi and J. Jabbra 2001, *Where Corruption Lives*, Bloomfield, CT: Kumarian, p. 217.

9　S. Rose-Ackerman 1978, *Corruption: A Study in Political Economy*, New York: Academic Press.

10　J. Brademas and F. Heimann 1998, 'Tackling International Corruption: No Longer Taboo', *Foreign Affairs* 77:5 (September/October), 17.

11　The following two databases provide comprehensive details about the publications that have appeared over the past decade: <http://www.worldbank.org/wbi/gac> and <http://www.transparency.org/publications/index.html>.

12　Toussaint [no initials provided] 1991, *African Communist*, 1st quarter, 31f.

13　J. T. Noonan Jr 1984, *Bribes*, New York: Macmillan, p. 542.

14　See unpublished paper delivered by Bishop Charles G. Palmer-Buckle on 'The Church's Role in the Fight Against Fraud' at Uganda Martyrs University in Nkozi on 8–10 April 1999.

15　R. Wraith and E. Simpkins 1970, 'Nepotism and Bribery in West Africa', in Heidenheimer, *Political Corruption*, p. 340. First published in 1963 in their book *Corruption in Developing Countries*, London: Allen & Unwin.

16　Leys, 'What is the Problem about Corruption?', p. 32.

17　M. Mbaku 1998, 'Bureaucratic and Political Corruption in Africa', in J. M. Mbaku, *Corruption and the Crisis of Institutional Reforms in Africa*, Lewiston, NY: Edwin Mellen, p. 66.

18　Ibid., p. 65.

19　Ibid. See Introduction to Part II, p. 158.

20　M. U. Ekpo 1979, 'Gift-Giving and Bureaucratic Corruption in Nigeria', in Mbaku, *Corruption and the Crisis of Institutional Reforms*, p. 182.

21　Derived from prebend, prebendary: 'In most English medieval cathedrals and collegiate churches, endowments were divided into separate portions in order to support members of the chapter. Each portion was known as a "prebend," because it supplied (*praebere*) a living to its holder, who also became known as a "prebendary"'. J. D. Douglas (ed.), *The New International Dictionary of the Christian Church*, Exeter: Paternoster, p. 797.

22　J. C. Andvig and O.-H. Fjeldstad 2000, *Research on Corruption: A Policy Oriented Survey*, unpublished final report commissioned by NORAD, p. 55.

23　Ibid., p. 66.

24　Ibid.

25 S. Andreske 1970, 'Kleptocracy as a System of Government in Africa', in Heidenheimer, *Political Corruption*, p. 353.

26 R. K. Merton 1968, *Social Theory and Social Structure*, New York: Free Press. Cited in R. Theobald 1990, *Corruption, Development and Underdevelopment*, London: Macmillan, pp. 108–10.

27 Merton, cited in Theobald, *Corruption, Development and Underdevelopment*, p. 110.

28 Ibid.

29 N. H. Leff 1970, 'Economic Development through Bureaucratic Development', in Heidenheimer, *Political Corruption*, pp. 510–20. First published in 1964 in *American Behavioral Scientist* 8:3 (November).

30 S. P. Huntington 1970, 'Modernization and Corruption', in Heidenheimer, *Political Corruption*, p. 498f. First published in 1968 in *Political Order in Changing Societies*. New Haven, CT: Yale University Press.

31 D. Osterfeld 1992, *Prosperity Versus Planning: How Government Stifles Economic Growth*, New York: Oxford University Press, pp. 204–17. Cited in Mbaku, *Corruption and the Crisis of Institutional Reforms*, p. 72.

32 Ekpo, in Mbaku, *Corruption and the Crisis of Institutional Reforms*, p. 170. For an elaboration of this counter-argument see R. M. Price 1975, *Society and Bureaucracy in Contemporary Ghana*, Berkeley: University of California Press.

33 J. Waterbury 1979, 'Endemic and Planned Corruption in a Monarchical Regime', in Ekpo, *Bureaucratic Corruption*, pp. 355–80.

34 G. C. S. Benson 1978, *Political Corruption in America*, Lexington, MA: Lexington Books, p. 214.

35 E. C. Banfield 1979, 'Corruption as a Feature of Governmental Organization', in Ekpo, *Bureaucratic Corruption*, pp. 75–99. First published in 1975 in *Journal of Law and Economics* 18 (December).

36 Ibid., p. 75.

37 Cf Rose-Ackerman, *Corruption*, p. 208f.

38 Ibid., p. 2.

39 Ibid., p. 218.

40 Klitgaard, *Controlling Corruption*, p. 74.

41 Ibid.

42 A. Shleifer and R. W. Vishny 1993, 'Corruption', *Quarterly Journal of Economics* CVIII, 599–616.

43 Klitgaard, *Controlling Corruption* (p. 72f.), notes some of these attempts.

44 Andvig and Fjeldstad, *Research on Corruption*, p. 118.

45 W. Martin 1990, *Public Choice Theory and Australian Agricultural Policy Reform*, Working Paper 90/2, National Centre for Development Studies, Australian National University, p. 2.

46 T. R. Dye 1995, *Understanding Public Policy*, Englewood Cliffs, NJ: Prentice Hall, Eighth edition, p. 35.

47 Martin, *Public Choice Theory*, p. 2.

48 Dye, *Understanding Public Policy*, p. 35.
49 Ibid., p. 37.
50 Montinola and Jackman, 'Sources of Corruption', p. 3.
51 Ibid.
52 See Rose-Ackerman, *Corruption and Government*.
53 Montinola and Jackman, 'Sources of Corruption', p. 3.
54 J. M. Mbaku 2000, *Bureaucratic and Political Corruption in Africa: The Public Choice Perspective*, Malabar, FL: Krieger, p. 159.
55 Ibid., p. 161.
56 Ibid., p. 162.
57 Ibid., p. 165f.
58 Montinola and Jackman, 'Sources of Corruption', p. 3.
59 P. Bardhan 1997, 'Corruption and Development: A Review of Issues', *Journal of Economic Literature* XXXV (September), 1341.
60 Ibid.
61 Girling, *Corruption, Capitalism and Democracy*, p. 8.
62 Tanzi, 'Corruption around the World'. Those reinventing the functionalist approach would include P. J. Beck and M. W. Maher 1986, 'A Comparison of Bribery and Bidding in Thin Markets', *Economic Letters* 20:1; D. Da Hsiang Lien 1985, 'A Note on Competitive Bribery Games', *Economic Letters* 22:4, and F. T. Lui 1985, 'An Equilibrium Queuing Model of Bribery', *Journal of Political Economy* 93 (August).
63 Tanzi, 'Corruption around the World', p. 44.
64 Ibid.
65 P. Le Billon 2003, 'Buying Peace or Fueling War: The Role of Corruption in Armed Conflicts', *Journal of International Development* 15, 413–36.
66 Ibid.
67 Ibid.
68 Ibid., p. 424.
69 Ibid.

3 Ways and means of fighting corruption

1 Leo W. J. C. Huberts 2000, 'Anti-Corruption Strategies: The Hong Kong Model in International Context', *Public Integrity* (Summer).
2 Robert Cameron 1991, *Public Policy, Politics: An Introduction for Southern African Students*, Cape Town: Oxford University Press, p. 130.
3 Ibid., p. 131.
4 Peter Self 1977, *Administrative Theories and Politics*, London: George Allen & Unwin, Second edition, p. 29f.
5 Dye, *Understanding Public Policy*, p. 27.
6 Ibid., p. 28.
7 H. A. Simon 1983, *Reason in Human Affairs*, Stanford, CA: Stanford University Press, p. 85.

8 Ibid., p. 34.

9 Ibid., p. 35.

10 Daniel W. Martin 1989, *The Guide to the Foundations of Public Administration*, New York and Basel: Marcel & Dekker, p. 360.

11 Klitgaard, *Controlling Corruption*, p. 25.

12 Ibid., p. 26.

13 Ibid.

14 Ibid.

15 Dye, *Understanding Public Policy*, p. 28. Kenneth Arrow, who won the Nobel Prize in Economic Sciences in 1972, has shown that 'it was impossible to find a reasonable and consistent procedure for any society to choose among conflicting alternatives' (see Walter P. Heller, Ross M. Starr and David A. Starrett (eds) 1986, *Social Choice and Public Decision-Making*, Cambridge: Cambridge University Press, p. 1). The complex problem of establishing social choice in the midst of competing values is elaborated upon by Arrow in a collection of his papers. See his *Social Choice and Justice*, Oxford: Basil Blackwell, 1984.

16 Ibid.

17 Ibid.

18 Self, *Administrative Theories*, p. 36. By 1983, when Simon delivered the Harry Camp Lectures at Stanford University in California, he was speaking of 'the limits of institutional rationality' and how 'human reason is less a tool for modeling and predicting the general equilibrium of the whole world system, or creating a massive general model that considers all variables at all times', than 'a first approximation, that people will act from self-interest' (Simon, *Reason in Human Affairs*, pp. 79, 105).

19 Self, *Administrative Theories*, p. 30.

20 B. W. Hogwood and L. A. Gunn 1984, *Policy Analysis for the Real World*, Oxford: Oxford University Press, p. 51.

21 Ibid.

22 Ibid.

23 Self, *Administrative Theories*, p. 34.

24 Simon's illustration is mentioned by Self, *Administrative Theories*, p. 35.

25 Ibid.

26 C. C. Holt and H. A. Simon 1982, 'Optimal Decision Rules for Production and Inventory Control', in H. A. Simon, *Models of Bounded Rationality: Economic Analysis and Public Policy*. Vol. 1, Cambridge, MA: Massachusetts Institute of Technology, p. 143.

27 Self, *Administrative Theories*, p. 35.

28 C. E. Lindblom 1959, 'The Science of Muddling Through', *Public Administration Review* 19.

29 Martin, *Guide to the Foundations*, p. 360.

30 Cameron, *Public Policy*, p. 139.

31 Dye, *Understanding Public Policy*, p. 31.

32 Ibid.

33 J. C. Pauw, G. Woods, J. A. van der Linde, D. Fourie and C. B. Visser (eds) 2000, *Managing Public Money: A System from the South*, London: Heinemann, p. 59.

34 Ibid.

35 Dye, *Understanding Public Policy*, p. 231.

36 A. Wildavsky, *Budgeting: A Comparative Theory of Budgetary Processes*, Boston, MA: Little, Brown & Co, p. 223.

37 Pauw et al., *Managing Public Money*, p. 60.

38 I. Abedian, T. Ajam and L. Walker 1997 [reprinted 1998], *Promises, Plans and Priorities: South Africa's Emerging Fiscal Structures*, Cape Town: IDASA, p. 14.

39 Self, *Administrative Theories*, p. 41.

40 Ibid., p. 43. Self mentions the example where 'one can analyse the probable effects of various subsidies upon the incomes of different groups of farmers, or the likely effects upon unemployment levels of alternative ways of allocating a given quantum of assistance. Since these factors can be measured according to a variety of methods and assumptions, full objectivity is impossible; but objectivity should at least increase as the view-point becomes more general and less influenced by special interests.'

41 Ibid.

42 Abedian et al., *Promises, Plans and Priorities*, p. 30.

43 Self, *Administrative Theories*, p. 43.

44 J. S. H. Gildenhuys 1993 [reprinted 1997], *Public Financial Management*, Pretoria: J. L. Van Schaik, p. 512.

45 J. C. Pauw 1999, 'Ethics and Budgets', in J. S. Wessels and J. C. Pauw, *Reflective Public Administration: Views from the South*, Cape Town: Oxford University Press, p. 205.

46 Abedian et al., *Promises, Plans and Priorities*, p. 107.

47 Ibid., p. 108.

48 Ibid., p. 109.

49 Pauw et al., *Managing Public Money*, p. 112. This argument is based on the assumption that benefits can be measured in terms of their priority status in the budget.

50 Ibid.

51 Pauw et al., *Managing Public Money*, p. 108.

52 W. van Ham 1998, *Transparency International (TI) – The International NGO Against Corruption: Strategic Positions Achieved and Challenges Ahead (A Case Study)*, Master of Business Administration dissertation submitted to Anglia Polytechnic University, p. 22.

53 J. Pope (ed.) 1996, *National Integrity Systems: The TI Source Book*, Berlin: Transparency International.

54 Ibid., p. 6.

55 See, for example, a publication of the Economic Development Institute of the World Bank written by K. M. Dye and R. Stapenhurst 1998, *Pillars*

of Integrity: The Importance of Supreme Audit Institutions in Curbing Corruption, Washington DC: World Bank. Note also the adaptation of the national integrity framework by the UN Global Programme Against Corruption.

56 Pope, *TI Source Book*, 2000 edition, p. 33.

57 Ibid.

58 Centre for Democracy and Governance 1998, *USAID Handbook for Fighting Corruption*, Technical Publication Series, Washington DC: USAID.

59 World Bank 2000, *Anti-Corruption in Transition: A Contribution to a Policy Debate*, Washington DC: World Bank.

60 United Nations 2001, *Anti-Corruption Tool Kit, Global Programme Against Corruption*, Centre for Crime Prevention, Office of Drug Control and Crime Prevention, United Nations, Vienna, Version 2 (September).

61 Ibid., p. 9.

62 A. Doig and S. McIvor, *The National Integrity System Concept and Practice*, Report by Transparency International for the Global Forum II on Fighting Corruption and Safeguarding Integrity, The Hague, Netherlands, 28–31 May 2001, p. 14.

63 Ibid.

64 M. Bryane, *The Rise and Fall of the Anti-Corruption Industry: Toward Second Generation Anti-Corruption Reforms in Central and Eastern Europe*, Linacre College, unpublished paper, p. 5.

65 Ibid., p. 6.

66 Ibid., p. 5.

67 Country Corruption Assessment Report, p. 11.

68 P. Rooke 2004, *The UN Convention against Corruption*, Global Corruption Report 2004, Transparency International, London: Pluto, p. 111.

69 Ibid.

70 Transparency International: Overcoming Obstacles to Enforcement of the OECD Convention on Combating Bribery of Foreign Public Officials: Report on Paris Meeting of 2–3 October 2003, Berlin, p. 1.

71 Ibid.

72 R. Batty 2002, 'Anti-Corruption Institutions and Practice in Southern Africa', in U. Zvekis (ed.), *Corruption and Anti-Corruption in Southern Africa*, Pretoria, UNODC: ROSA, p. 57.

73 Ibid.

74 Ibid.

75 See text in A. T. Muna 2003, *The African Union Convention on Preventing and Combating Corruption and Related Offences*, Berlin: Transparency International, pp. 38–48.

76 Wildavsky, *Budgeting*, p. 320.

77 T. Wing Lo 1993, *Corruption and Politics in Hong Kong and China*, Milton Keynes, Bucks: Open University Press, p. 80.

78 Bertrand de Speville 1997, *Hong Kong: Policy Initiatives Against Corruption*, Development Centre Studies, Paris: OECD, p. 12.

79 Lo, *Corruption and Politics*, p. 80.

80 Ibid., p. 82.

81 De Speville, *Hong Kong: Policy Initiatives*, p. 16.

82 Lo, *Corruption and Politics*, p. 86.

83 Ibid., p. 87.

84 Ibid., p. 88.

85 Ibid., p. 91.

86 De Speville, *Hong Kong: Policy Initiatives*, p. 21.

87 Ibid.

88 Ibid., p. 22. See ICAC Ordinance, Section 5(2).

89 Ibid., p. 45.

90 Richard C. LaMagna, *Changing a Culture of Corruption: How Hong Kong's Independent Commission Against Corruption Succeeded in Furthering a Culture of Lawfulness*, Working Group on Crime Monograph Series, June 1999, National Strategy Information Centre, Washington DC.

91 Ibid., p. 63.

92 Leo W. J. C. Huberts, 'Anti-Corruption Strategies: The Hong Kong Model in International Context', *Public Integrity*, Summer 2000, p. 216 and Klitgaard, *Controlling Corruption*, p. 115.

93 LaMagna, *Changing a Culture*, p. 23.

94 Huberts, *Anti-Corruption Strategies*, p. 217.

95 ICAC Review Committee Report, 1994. Cited in de Speville, *Hong Kong: Policy Initiatives*, p. 60.

96 LaMagna, *Changing a Culture*, p. 24.

97 A. L. Nin, *What ICAC has done for Hong Kong and How?* Paper presented at International Anti Corruption Roundtable, Pretoria, 31 May–2 June 2000, p. 3.

98 Dye, *Understanding Public Policy*, p. ix.

4 Costs and benefits of fighting corruption

1 This assumption is based on conclusions reached in an earlier study upon which this chapter is substantially based. See my 'Fighting Corruption in the South African Public Sector with special reference to Costs and Impact', unpublished doctoral dissertation, University of South Africa, 2005.

2 This is a daily newspaper published in the South African capital.

3 Klitgaard, *Controlling Corruption*.

4 In my doctoral study (note 1 above), I have given this gap in corruption studies more attention. See especially pp. 36–40.

5 21 September 2004.

6 See the discussion on national integrity systems in Chapter 3.

7 Pauw et al., *Managing Public Money*.

8 F. Anechiarico and James B. Jacobs 1996, *The Pursuit of Absolute Integrity: How Corruption Control Makes Government Ineffective* (Chicago: University of Chicago Press). See also P. K. Howard 1994, *The Death of Common Sense: How Law is Suffocating America* (New York: Warner Books).

9 Klitgaard, *Controlling Corruption*, pp. 15–24.

10 Jon S. T. Quah 2001, 'Combating Corruption in the Asia Pacific Region', in Gerald E. Caiden, O. P. Dwivedi and Joseph Jabbra (eds) 2001, *Where Corruption Lives*, Bloomfield, CT: Kumarian Press, p. 131.

11 Ibid., p. 142.

5 A South African case study

1 V. G. Hilliard and H. F. Wissink 2001, 'Understanding Corruption in the South African Public Sector', in Caiden et al., *Where Corruption Lives*.

2 Unpublished paper, Pretoria, August 1995. Ginwala was herself more recently implicated in the failings of the South African government under the leadership of Mandela's successor, Thabo Mbeki, whom she exonerated from blame after he suspended a key justice department official. Mbeki was eventually asked by his party to step down from office in 2008 and he duly obliged.

3 T. Lodge 1997, *Political Corruption in South Africa*, University of the Witwatersrand: Institute for Advanced Social Research, Paper No. 425 (August), p. 6.

4 A. Seegers 1993, 'Toward An Understanding Of The Afrikanerization Of The South African State', *Africa* 63(4). Cited in Lodge, *Political Corruption*.

5 J. N. N. Cloete 1978, 'The Bureaucracy', in A. de Crispigny and R. Schire 1978, *The Government and Politics of South Africa*, Cape Town: Juta & Co., p. 74.

6 Lodge, *Political Corruption*, p. 6f.

7 J. Hyslop 2003, 'Political Corruption: Before and After Apartheid', Wits Institute for Social and Economic Research Annual Workshop, University of the Witwatersrand, Johannesburg, 14–18 July 2003.

8 A. Boraine 1995, 'Parliamentarians, Corruption and Human Rights Abuse'. Paper presented at the Africa Leadership Forum, Pretoria, August 1995, p. 8.

9 E. Rhoodie 1983, *The Real Information Scandal*, Pretoria: Orbis SA, p. 320.

10 H. Van Vuuren 2003, *National Integrity Systems*, TI Country Study Report: South Africa 2003 (draft), unpublished, p. 9.

11 Rhoodie, *The Real Information Scandal*, p. 893.

12 *Finance Week*, 24 September 1999, p. 10.

13 C. Bauer 2000, 'Public Sector Corruption and its Control in South Africa', in K. R. (Sr) Hope and B. C. Chikulo, *Corruption and Development in Africa: Lessons from Country Case-Studies*. Houndmills, Hampshire:

Macmillan, p. 222. Bauer offers a detailed discussion of the Pickard and Van den Heever Commissions' findings (see pp. 220–27).

14 Van Vuuren, *National Integrity Systems*, p. 8.

15 *The Star*, 16 April 1993; 29 September 1993; 1 October 1993; 19 November 1993.

16 Ibid.

17 S. Booysen 2001, 'Transitions and Trends in Policymaking in Democratic South Africa', *Journal of Public Administration* 36:2 (June), 131.

18 Ibid.

19 Ann Bernstein 1999, *Policy-Making in a New Democracy: South Africa's Challenges for the 21st Century*, Johannesburg: Centre for Development and Enterprise (August), p. 19.

20 M. Wiechers 1995, 'The Caring/Benefactor State and its Administration', *Journal of Public Administration* 30:4 (December), 236.

21 A. Habib and H. Kotze 2003, 'Civil Society, Governance and Development in an Era of Globalization: The South African Case', in G. Mhone and O. Edigheji (eds), *Governance in the New South Africa: The Challenges of Globalization*, Cape Town: University of Cape Town Press, p. 253.

22 Ibid., p. 256.

23 G. Houston and Y. Muthien 2000, 'South Africa: A Transformative State?', in Y. G. Muthien, M. M. Khosa and B. M. Mugubane (eds), *Democracy and Governance Review: Mandela's Legacy 1994–1999*, Pretoria: HSRC, p. 55.

24 Ibid.

25 E. Omano 2003, 'State-Society Relations in Post-Apartheid South Africa: The Challenges of Globalization on Co-operative Governance', in Mhone and Edigheji, *Governance in the New South Africa*, p. 70.

26 Bernstein, *Policy-Making in a New Democracy*, pp. 87–97.

27 Booysen, 'Transitions and Trends', p. 128.

28 Ibid., p. 135.

29 Bernstein, *Policy-Making in a New Democracy*, p. 22.

30 Ibid., p. 20.

31 Ibid.

32 Ibid.

33 Ibid.

34 Booysen, 'Transitions and Trends', p. 129.

35 Ibid., p. 135.

36 Ibid., p. 133.

37 Ibid., p. 137.

38 Habib and Kotze, 'Civil Society', p. 266.

39 Ibid., p. 268.

40 Bernstein, *Policy-Making in a New Democracy*, p. 23.

41 S. Vorster (ed.) 1998, *Corruption Barometer 1994–1998*, Cape Town: National Party Federal Council. The New National Party has now joined the ANC!

42 Ibid., p. 4.

43 Ibid., p. 108.

44 Ibid., p. 4.

45 Ibid., p. 8.

46 R. Mattes and C. Africa 1999, 'Corruption – The Attitudinal Component: Tracking Public Perceptions of Official Corruption in South Africa, 1995–1998'. Paper presented at the 9th International Anti-Corruption Conference, Durban, 12 October 1999.

47 Ibid., p. 5f.

48 L. Camerer 2001, *Corruption in South Africa: Results of an Expert Panel Survey*, Institute for Security Studies Monograph Series No. 65, Pretoria: Institute for Security Studies.

49 Ibid., p. 31.

50 Ibid., p. 46.

51 C. Alan, R. Mattes and U. Millie 2002, *Government Corruption Seen from the Inside: A Survey of Public Officials' Perceptions of Corruption in the Eastern Cape*, PSAM Research Series No. 1, Public Service Accountability Monitor, Rhodes University, Grahamstown.

52 Ibid., p. vi.

53 Van Vuuren, *National Integrity Systems*, p. 9.

54 Lodge, *Political Corruption*, p. 18.

55 See Act No. 108 of 1996, sections 32, 33 and 195.

56 See a full discussion of this theme in the *TI Source Book 2000*, pp. 119–36.

57 Lodge, *Political Corruption*, p. 15.

58 TI 1997, *Corruption and Good Governance*, Braamfontein: Transparency South Africa, 1997, p. 23 (unpublished). See also Court's decision not to prosecute in charges of defamation brought by the former minister against the *Mail and Guardian*, 13–19 August 2004.

59 25 January 1996.

60 *Sunday Times*, 9 June 1996. See the detailed discussion of the Sarafina 2 scandal in A. Venter 1998, 'The Sarafina 2 Case: Evasion of Ministerial Responsibility to Parliament', *Journal of Public Administration* 33:2 (June), 87–105.

61 Van Vuuren, *National Integrity Systems*, p. 10.

62 Ibid.

63 T. Lodge 2003, 'Southern Africa', in R. Hodess (ed.) 2003, *TI Global Corruption Report 2003*, Berlin: Transparency International, p. 253.

64 Van Vuuren, *National Integrity Systems*, p. 11.

65 TI 1995, *Corruption Perceptions Index*, Berlin: Transparency International.

66 'Proposal for a Campaign against Corruption: Report to Minister A. Omar', July 1998, Department of Justice, unmarked, unpublished. Office of the Public Service Commission (OPSC) File No. 343/98.

67 Minutes of Cabinet meeting, 8 October 1997.

68 Minutes of Cabinet meeting, 23 September 1999.

69 Report to Minister Omar, p. 2.

70 Ibid., p. 11.
71 Office of the Public Service Commission, Ethics Division, Pretoria, File No. 343/153.
72 T. Mbeki 1999, 'Keynote Address: Fighting Corruption in South Africa', in S. Sangweni and D. Balia (eds), *Fighting Corruption: Strategies for Prevention*, Pretoria: Unisa Press, p. 11.
73 Ibid., pp. 21–4.
74 Ibid., p. 166.
75 Ibid., p. 169.
76 See, for example, *Sunday Times*, 15 November 1998.
77 B. Adair, 'Consultant's Report 1999', in Sangweni and Balia, *Fighting Corruption*, p. 25.
78 Ibid., p. 47.
79 Opening Address to Parliament, 1999.
80 TI 1997, *Corruption and Good Governance*, Transparency South Africa, Braamfontein (unpublished).
81 'Civil Society and Mobilization against Corruption', Unpublished paper presented at the Africa Leadership Forum Seminar on Corruption, Democracy and Human Rights Abuse in Southern Africa, 31 July–2 August 1995, p. 2.
82 Sangweni and Balia, *Fighting Corruption*, p. 4.
83 *Towards an Integrated Anti-Corruption Strategy*, National Civil Society Anti-Corruption Report, 25 August 2000, Willow Park, Johannesburg: Transparency South Africa.
84 *Anti Corruption Tool Kit*, p. 74.
85 De Speville, *Hong Kong: Policy Initiatives*, p. 58.
86 OPSC/343/127.

6 Bribery and the Bible

1 Deontology is seen as problematic by many as it tends to focus too strongly on the ethical act and most deontologists believe that 'there are universal rules that provide standards of right and wrong behaviour', like the rule that we should not lie. This leads to an 'un-reflexive compliance to rules' which 'removes the moral dilemma' and causes us to be desensitized to our own moral judgment. This attempt to 'bureaucratize morality leads to its displacement' as the ethics of the acts get separated from the ethics of the agent, to the neglect of the agent. (David Knights and Majella O'Leary 2006, 'Leadership, Ethics and Responsibility to the Other', *Journal of Business Ethics* (2006) 67:125–137, p. 130.
2 Tremper Longman III 2006, *Proverbs*, Grand Rapids, MI: Baker Academic, p. 552.
3 Kathleen A. Farmer 1991, *Who Knows What Is Good*, Grand Rapids, MI: Eerdmans, p. 88.
4 See also Matt. 21.12–13, John 2.14–16.

5 John H. Elliot 1996, 'Patronage and Clientage', in Richard Rohrbaugh (ed.), *The Social Sciences and New Testament Interpretation*, Peabody, MA: Hendrickson, p. 146.

6 Bruce J. Malina and Richard L. Rohrbaugh 1992, *Social Science Commentary on the Synoptic Gospels*, Minneapolis, MN: Fortress, p. 75.

7 Elliot, 'Patronage and Clientage', p. 152.

8 Malina, Bruce J. 1988, 'Patron and Client: The Analogy behind Synoptic Theology', *Forum* 4:1, 2–32.

9 John T. Noonan Jr. 1984, *Bribes*, Berkeley and Los Angeles: University of California Press, p. 59. The Judicial Court at Nisibis in Mesopotamia is the site of a similar account as told by a H. B. Tristam in a nineteenth-century report (see Malina and Rohrbaugh, *Social Science Commentary on the Synoptic Gospels*, p. 381):

> Opposite the entrance sat the Cadi, half buried in cushions, and surrounded by secretaries. The front of the hall was crowded with people, each demanding that his case would be heard first. The wise ones whispered to the secretaries and slipped over bribes, and had their business quickly dispatched. In the meanwhile, a poor woman broke through the orderly proceedings with loud cries for justice. She was sternly bidden to be quiet, and reproachfully told that she came every day. 'And so I will do,' she loudly exclaimed, 'until the Cadi hears my case.' At length, at the end of the session, the Cadi impatiently asked, 'What does the woman want?' Her story was soon told. The tax collector was demanding payment from her, although her only son was on military service. The case was quickly decided and her patience was rewarded. If she had had money to pay a clerk she would have obtained justice much sooner.

10 Halvor Moxnes 1988, *The Economy of the Kingdom*, Philadelphia, PA: Fortress, p. 130.

11 Moxnes, *Economy of the Kingdom*, p. 129.

12 Ibid., p. 133.

13 Gerd Theissen 1999, *The Religion of the Earliest Churches*, Minneapolis, MN: Fortress, p. 93.

14 *Jewish Ethicist*, weekly online advice provided by Rabbi Dr Asher Meir of the Business Ethics Centre of Jerusalem, 14 March 2008, <http://www.besr.org>.

15 Ruth Messinger, 'Judaism, Corruption and American Jewish World Service', American Jewish World Service, 30 May 2001 (unpublished paper).

16 *Jewish Ethicist*, 14 March 2008.

17 Rafik Issa Beekun 1997, *Islamic Business Ethics*, International Institute of Islamic Thought: Herndon, Virginia.

18 Islam QA, 2 March 1429–9 March 2008, <http://www.islam-qa.com>.

19 Islam QA.

20 Sayed Othman Alhabshi 1996, *Definition of Bribery according to Islam*, Institute of Islamic Understanding, Malaysia, unpublished paper, 2 November 1996, p. 3.
21 Alhabshi, *Definition of Bribery*, p. 3.
22 Albert Nolan 2006, *Jesus Today: A Spirituality of Radical Freedom*, Cape Town: Double Story, p. 57.
23 Ibid., *Jesus Today*, p. 58.

7 What can churches do?

1 M. Padlam 2001, 'Corruption and Religion: Adding to the Economic Model', *Kyklos*, 54, 383–414.
2 H. Marquette and G. Singh, 'Whither Morality? Disciplinary Secularism in the Political Economy of Corruption in Developing Countries', University of Birmingham, paper prepared for the 102nd American Political Science Association Annual Meeting, Philadelphia, 31 August–2 September 2006, p. 10.
3 C. North and C. Gwin 2006, *Religion, Corruption, and the Rule of Law* (July), see <http://www. religionomics.com>.
4 D. Beets 2007, 'International Corruption and Religion: An Empirical Examination', *Journal of Global Ethics*, 3:1.
5 D. Serra 2006, 'Empirical Determinants of Corruption: A Sensitivity Analysis', *Public Choice*, 126, 225–56.
6 Pontifical Council for Justice and Peace, *The Fight Against Corruption*, 21 September 2006, <http://www.vatican.va/roman_curia/pontifical_councils/justpeace/documents/rc_pc_justpeace_doc_20060921_lotta-corruzione_en.html>.
7 M. Ramaite 1999, 'Corruption versus Good Administration of Public Affairs', in Sangweni and Balia, *Fighting Corruption*, p. 161.
8 Corruption Act No. 94 of 1992, Government Gazette, Cape Town. See chapter 1 of this study for fuller discussion on the definition of corruption.
9 Ramaite, 'Corruption versus Good Administration', p. 62.
10 Ibid.
11 See discussion on legislative reforms in *TI Source Book 2000*, pp. 269–85.
12 See Chapter 6 of Corruption Act 1992.
13 De Sardan, 'A Moral Economy of Corruption in Africa?', 48.
14 Section 32(1) of the South African Constitution, Pretoria, 1996.
15 Visit <http://www.opendemocracy.org.za>.
16 D. S. Mukalani 2002, 'Access to Information Legislation in Africa', unpublished paper presented at Access to Information Seminar in Hua Hin, Thailand, 3 March 2002.
17 R. Calland 2001, 'Access to Information: Modern South Africa and Globalization'. Paper presented at seminar on Freedom of Information

in Central and Eastern Europe, Bucharest, Romania, 3–5 October 2001 (unpublished).

18 R. Hodess (ed.) 2001, *Global Corruption Report 2001*, Berlin: Transparency International, p. 20.

19 See the publication by R. Calland and G. Dehn 2004, *Whistle-Blowing Around the World*, Cape Town: Open Democracy Advice Centre.

20 Hodess, *Global Corruption Report 2001*, p. 61.

21 See Calland and Dehn, *Whistle-Blowing Around the World*.

22 Calland and Dehn, Introduction, *Whistle-Blowing Around the World*, p. 10.

23 V. Johnson 2004, 'Public Deception in Cape Town: Story of An Insider Witness', in Calland and Dehn, *Whistle-Blowing Around the World*, p. 52.

24 R. Douglas and M. Jones 1996, *Administrative Law: Commentary and Materials*, Second edition, Annandale: Federation Press, p. 141.

25 Ibid., p. 137.

26 De Sardan, 'A Moral Economy of Corruption in Africa, p. 33.

27 Ibid.

28 'Mass Media and the Campaign against Corruption', paper presented at the Africa Leadership Forum Conference, Midrand, 1 August 1995.

29 Ibid.

30 B. Peters 2003, 'The Media's Role: Covering or Covering Up Corruption?', in Hodess, *Global Corruption Report 2003*, p. 45.

31 Van Vuuren, *National Integrity Systems*, p. 31.

32 Ibid.

33 Ibid.

34 *TI Source Book 2000*, p. 127.

35 Ibid.

36 *Anti-Corruption Tool Kit*, Global Programme Against Corruption, Version 1, p. 121.

37 Ibid.

38 Country Corruption Assessment Report, p. 84.

39 Ibid., p. 85.

40 *Anti-Corruption Tool Kit*, p. 122.

41 Marcel Mauss 1990, *The Gift*, London: W. W. Norton, pp. 82–3.

Index